IN THE HOPE
OF HIS
COMING

Studies In Christian Unity

edited by
Emmanuel Maria Heufelder, O.S.B.

Translated by Otto M. Knab

FIDES PUBLISHERS, INC.
NOTRE DAME, INDIANA

© *Copyright:* 1964, Fides Publishers, Inc.
Notre Dame, Indiana

Nihil Obstat: Louis J. Putz, C.S.C.
University of Notre Dame

Imprimatur: Leo A. Pursley, D.D.
Bishop of Fort Wayne-South Bend

Library of Congress Catalog Card Number: 64-23520

A translation of the series *Das Alle Eins Seien,* published from 1959
to 1962 by Paulus Verlag, Recklinghausen, Germany.

Manufactured in the United States of America

INTRODUCTION

Abbot Emmanuel Heufelder of Niederalteich Abbey in Bavaria has offered his abbey and his Benedictine hospitality for the promotion of Christian unity. Similar undertakings have occurred in Belgium at the Chevetogne Priory and in France at the Protestant community of Taizé. This, in itself, is a sign of the times. The spirit of reunion is reaching the high-water mark. It is to further this movement that Abbot Emmanuel Heufelder collected this series of essays to treat the questions that are in the forefront of the reunion of Christendom. A wider public can thus share in the concerns and preoccupations of those who are working for the reunion of all Christians.

The book that has resulted is not offering answers to the questions that are asked by an increasing number of people, but the different chapters do offer a background to these questions so that they can be discussed fruitfully and meaningfully. The book is meant to create an atmosphere of mind and heart in which a fruitful encounter between separated Christians will be possible.

The authors place themselves fully in the service of the great goals which Pope John XXIII summarized in the words he spoke with a view to the Council he had summoned: "The main aim of this Council is to further an increase of the Catholic faith, a salutary renewal of morality among the Christian people, and the adaptation of the discipline of the Church to the necessities of our times."

Although the chapters were written before the convening of the Council, they have lost none of their cogency and urgency. They offer a precious background to the discussion and the decisions that are forthcoming from the Council sessions. As a matter of fact, it might be said that if the Council is to bear fruit, more and more of the faithful need to be in the spirit of the Council. The spirit of the genial Pope John must prevail not only in the Council but among all the faithful if the reunion will eventually take place in God's good time. That spirit was expressed by the late Holy Father when he addressed to the separated Christians "a gentle invitation to seek and achieve that unity for which Jesus Christ implored his father in such ardent prayers."

At this point of our historical perspective we can see how tragic was the failure on the part of fifteenth and sixteenth century Churchmen not to have heeded the universal clamor for a reform of the Church in head and members. It split Christendom into fragments that hurt the whole cause of Christ's Church. It has taken four centuries to repair this mistake. In order that greater progress be made in reuniting the various branches of the Christian people, a deeper awareness of the problem is necessary at the grassroots level.

In the sixteenth century there was more concentration on reform of the head and not enough on reform of the members. This caused the split of Christendom into innumerable fragments. Each local community, each reformer went his own way without thought of the consequences that this would have for future generations. For Christian unity to become a reality, the reform of each segment is necessary. Every separate Christian community has to examine itself on its spirit of charity and its motivation, each community must strike its breast with a genuine "mea culpa" together with the Vatican Council which by its very reform spirit is saying its "mea maxima culpa."

The world at large is fast moving toward a geographic, economic, technological, and political unity. Oceans are capable of being spanned in a matter of hours; a crisis in any one country spells trouble for all countries; scientists speak a common language; the United Nations, whatever its weaknesses, is becoming a fact and a necessity. The Church cannot stay aloof from this movement toward unity. As a matter of fact, the Church must give it a soul, the love necessary to make this striving toward unity a meaningful effort. Certainly this world movement toward unity is not only an added reason for Christian unity, but even a powerful stimulus.

Nevertheless, the obstacles toward unity are real and must be faced with courage and wisdom. Efforts toward a reform and toward unity have been in the wind for at least half a century since the Pontificate of Leo XIII, but greater and more intense progress must be made if the needs of the world are to be helped by the Christian leaven. The reform movement must not remain in the Council sessions, it must not be the exclusive preoccupation of theologians, it must be shared by all of the Christian people.

A first step, obviously, is the recognition of one another as Christian people, as possessors of Christian values whatever our denomination. Instead of concentrating on our separateness, Pope John emphasized our brotherly dimension. This is a first step. We must be willing to recognize one another as heirs to the Kingdom. A second step is to appreciate one another's contribution and one another's problems. It seems to me that we are entering now into this phase of the ecumenical movement. Most of the writing and discussing is in this area. It seems that this is the contribution that this book seeks to make. The third step will be the final step of helping one another to achieve a measure of unity.

It is important that we undertake to help the cause of Christian unity in the light of modern developments and modern needs, rather than in the spirit of the sixteenth or seventeenth century. Wars were fought and the blood of martyrs was shed in order to impose on those who disagreed a partial solution, a one-sided reform. Christian charity demands that we be willing to admit mistakes on all sides, that we be willing to learn from all concerned, that we have at heart the main concern of Christ "that all may be one." A common desire, an ardent prayer, mutual respect is already a major change of heart. Before we can plan a reunion, all concerned must want it with all their hearts. Perhaps the present book can help to generate this spirit. With this hope these chapters are offered to the general public.

Louis J. Putz, C.S.C.
University of Notre Dame

CONTENTS

1

Joseph Lortz | # CHRISTIAN DISUNITY AND HOW TO SPEAK ABOUT IT

How to Speak About Christian Disunity

OF THE TWO themes stated in the title, the second one shall be treated first. It is the more important one of the two. Much richer in consequences than a person's expressions and questions is the fundamental attitude that determines his thinking.

Christians should speak about things Christian only as committed men and women; that is to say, only from religious motives. For Christians, this can mean only one thing: as people committed to love. Therefore, we cannot speak abstractly of the disunity of Christianity. We must think and speak as Christ did: "That all may be one . . . that the world may believe that thou hast sent me" (John 17: 21). A word full of urgent pleading to the Father, but also one of forewarning to us, spoken by our Lord on the eve of His passion. The unity of Christians among themselves is here projected as the condition for the belief of the world in Jesus Christ— the disunity of Christians being the cause of unbelief.

The facts are obvious today: Christianity is divided within itself. Since the origin of that division in centuries long past, unbelief has increased in and outside our Churches in frightening proportions. We have known this for some time. But we have accepted it and take it for granted. And this, precisely, is what is wrong. If we take ourselves and Christianity seriously, all disunity must make us uneasy; the task of reunion, or at least the preparation for it, must burn in our conscience.

We, the divided disciples of Christ, should often reflect on this fact before the tabernacle. There an examination of conscience may indeed take on a special urgency. We may hope that it will be under a special blessing.

Examination of conscience is always accusation—accusation against oneself.

It can very well be, however, that mixed into this self-accusation are elements which objectively demand that a part of the guilt and responsibility must be ascribed to our brother. We can make such judgments only if we do so in a spirit of charity, avoiding all hypocrisy.

The most important element is this—that we speak to one another in the right disposition. This is more important than any single point we may discuss or question. Brothers, Catholic or Protestant, let us be one in the Lord!

Let us not deceive ourselves. Let us listen carefully to what the words mean. The Lord has demanded from us an incomprehensible unity: "As thou, Father, in me and I in thee." And He asked this unity not only for the future, for the time of His second coming when we shall see Him face to face; He asked it for this time in which we see only by faith. For He even makes our unity the prerequisite for the faith of the world: "that the world may believe that thou hast sent me."

We are not "one" as long as we believe different and contradictory things about the Church, the ministry, the priesthood. Since the division between the Eastern and Western Church in the eleventh century, but in the deeper meaning of a real schism at least since the sixteenth century, Christianity has been rent apart and torn. There can be no doubt that this development was contrary to the will of the Lord. And it still is. This event of history, the division of Christianity, is not past, it is present. It concerns us all, all Christians here and now. Therefore, we cannot speak about the Reformation, whether it be to adherents of our own faith or with our separated brethren, as though we were not personally involved. We are speaking about something in which we have become vitally involved through our fathers, through our Church.

And whatever anyone may think of the Reformation—how highly he may praise it as a cleansing of the Temple, a purification of the Word—he cannot forget as a Christian that the immediate consequence of it was a disunited Christendom. And that means, as we saw, the actual reversal of our Lord's last wish—irrespective of what Luther and Zwingli and Calvin may have desired deep in their hearts. After all, they wanted purification, they wanted the will of the Lord fulfilled in *one* Church. But what came was a split, and many denominations.

Thus, every discussion of the Reformation stands in a special way under the one word which constitutes the main theme of the New Testament: *Metanoia,* or the call to penance, to a change of heart. A call to whom? What a question for a Christian, to whom the humility of the publican has been held up once and for all as *the* Christian attitude—and who should love his brother as himself!

The first thing that is necessary therefore is that we, that all, that at least many more Christians than now do, recognize the burden, the misery, the guilt of Christian disunity; that the number of Christians who, though knowing the fact of this division, are not bothered by it, be reduced so that more and more Christians will recognize this situation, if not through consciousness of a kind of deep family guilt, at least as awareness of a continuing burden and a weakening of the Church.

This is a serious problem, for we are not yet at the point where union with our separated brethren is the official central concern of our Church everywhere.

Whether our unyielding attitude is caused by intellectual inertia or little faith, an attachment to the past or a lack of historical and theological understanding, is of minor importance. The fact of a certain practical indolence in matters of this kind affects the well-being of the Church in its very nature. All in the Church should therefore join us in this earnest examination of conscience.

The fullness of time was totally realized *once:* when God sent His Son in the flesh (Rom. 8: 3). But since then, this fullness of time, in an intrinsic sense, has been and is a *continuous* reality. Salvation is offered to us continually, always.

And yet it is axiomatic that the works of God take place in the order of right measure and right time (Rom. 12: 3). So also in the historical currents wherein our salvation must be worked out, there are favored places and appointed hours. Sometimes the hour for a certain task is ripe: it enters into its appointed hour, its *kairos*.[1]

---

1. The Greek word connotes not only the meaning of "right season," "proper time," but it is used in Holy Scripture in the context of preordained time, e.g. in Rom. 13: 11; Apoc. 1: 3. (Translator's note.)

The "appointed hour" of an idea capable of changing fate itself cannot be prolonged at will; its consummation cannot be delayed without impunity.

As happens in human history, the breakup in the sixteenth century was typically marked by lack of charity and by enmity. Holy zeal for the house of God as well as holy anger was involved on both sides, but down to our own days neither side has succeeded in really illuminating its arguments. The inevitable discussions, however much they were carried out in the line of duty, often violated the principal law of Christian life and growth: that of love. And so it is understandable that the fruits of love, namely unity and harmony, were absent.

If we want to do better today, we must speak to each other in love, out of a positive tolerance which, in the spirit of Christian doctrine, aims for unity. It must be an attitude capable of respect for the tremendous phenomenon of the Reformation, which has left its imprint on the existence of all mankind. We must have respect even for one of the Reformation's consequences—the division of Christianity; respect, because even this central event of modern history, by which humanity as a whole has been directly or indirectly effected, lies in the hands of the Father without whom nothing can occur.

The Church is missionary by its very nature. Every word she utters in her capacity as church must serve the spreading of the kingdom of God, that is to say: the salvation of the world, of all men. The same holds true of every Christian whenever he speaks in the Church's service. In this spirit I want to speak in the following pages to both Catholics and to our brothers that are separated from us.

I do not forget that in the letter to Timothy the instruction is given to preach the word in season and out of season (2 Tim. 4: 2). To the Church is entrusted the *depositum fidei,* the deposit of the faith. She is not at liberty to surrender any of it, because she is not its master. Therefore she has no choice but to be dogmatically intolerant, lest she betray her trust. In the fullness of her claim on the truth there is no room, not even a point of departure, for relativism of any kind.

Still, who could have shown a more considerate attitude and discretion towards the demands of his brothers' conscience, whether they were pagans or Jews, than Paul? The dogmatic intolerance he preached ("But even if . . . an angel from heaven should preach a gospel to you other than that which we have preached to you, let him be anathema!" Gal. 1: 8), this intolerance which the Church inherited from the Lord and from him, is essentially joined to a positive tolerance—a tolerance which recognizes in the one unalterable doctrine the mystery of the various and varying ways of grace.

Whenever a Catholic becomes aware of the fullness of faith in his Church; whenever, through great demonstrations of public worship where the Church prays as one body, he experiences the power of the Church's faith; whenever he observes the awakening of a new renewal movement in the history of the Church, as in a council, his heart widens. But we must not think that this is all there is of reality. On the contrary, the reality of the world is unbelief. The Bible says this, experience confirms it. And unbelief, when compared to belief, is undoubtedly still on the increase.

How to counteract this is not the subject of our discussion. There are many causes for unbelief. But of all these reasons, there is none that advances unbelief more, and is still furthering it, than our Christian disunion. (The warning of our Lord is here borne out.) For what in the final analysis, does the schism in Christianity mean? It means that the *one* message of Jesus Christ, the *one* doctrine of salvation, *the* truth is being preached by different Churches, in different, mutually contradictory ways.

Let us leave aside for a moment the consoling, indeed saving, fact that the divided denominations still have an important spiritual heritage in common. I shall speak about that later. Let us simply confess: through the Christian schism the persuasive power of the word of God has been effectively diminished. Because of the schism, the ability of modern man even to conceive of truth as one, has been decisively weakened. Relativism, the most serious of mankind's spiritual diseases and due, at least in part to the disunion of Christians, is still being fostered in our own day.

What can the truth of Christianity mean to unbelievers when they see, century after century, this so-called truth variously presented in Catholic, Lutheran, Calvinist versions, or in any one of the more than two hundred reformed Christian sects?

But if we deplore disunity, we have to know what kind of unity we are seeking. Unity is a complex thing. What is the unity of those who on the word of the Apostles believe in the Lord? Wherein does the unity of this message and that of the community created by it, the unity of the Church, consist?

This unity is Jesus Christ. And this all-embracing answer we must have constantly before our eyes when we speak of Christian unity.

But "be sober, be watchful!" (1 Pet. 5: 8.) This answer does not suffice after all. "What do you think of the Christ?" (Matt. 22: 42.) The Gospel and the two thousand years of its history tell us that various things can be understood by the same name. Inconceivably rich as this word "Jesus Christ" is, what really matters is that we interpret it correctly, not as flesh and blood would tell us, but as the Father has revealed it (Matt. 16: 17).

Certainly, the unity of Christianity, of Christendom, of the Church is a mystery; for the Church is the mystical body of the One in whom we profess the mystery of salvation through the incarnation of God.

At the same time, the Church preaches God's *general* intent for man's salvation. But again we have the pleading voice of Christ beseeching the Father for the true unity of the Church; one is tempted to say He contends with God for this. The facts of world and religious history provide such drastic proof for the disunity of religion throughout the world that the vision of true unity of faith and adoration must appear utopian to sober reasoning. Even within Christianity itself, and since its earliest days, the unity of the faithful has been shockingly noticeable by its absence.

Thus, the unity of the Church is a mystery. The various books of Holy Scripture demonstrate impressively that the unity of their doctrine can be said to exist only in a very qualified sense. It is simply impossible to speak of this unity as though there were for every text, for every question that arises from the word of God, ready-made theoretical formulas which, connected together, provide a seamless garment of meaning for Holy Scripture.

It is of course true that the Gospel is not just symbolic

language. It is truth which can be recognized, and is unchangeable in its essence. But it is by no means conceptually uniform. The theology that is contained in the Bible, monastic theology, the theology of liturgy, the theologies of St. Thomas and St. Bonaventure prove to us the doctrine that God must be professed as the Unknown. All these authorities emphatically remind us of the limitations of abstract theology and warn us how restrained we must be in making accusations of fideism.[2]

Both Holy Scripture and Christianity in its early and medieval periods, although displaying an essential unity, are full of legitimate tensions. Through the advent of the Logos, the Word made flesh, only that which is essential is protected from falling into sin and error. This is a universal law from which there is no exception. The attempt to find exceptions only creates new contradictions. How could one express our concept of the Church today and the concrete claim to power of a Boniface VIII; the concept of papal primacy and that of the collegiality of the Apostles all in *one* formula.

And let us remember the powerful heresies of the first centuries, from the Church of Marcion to Arianism and the Donatists, and the world-wide movements of Nestorianism and Monophysitism.

Thus the unity of the Church in history corresponds to the mystery of its form which, although visible, is nevertheless primarily a matter of faith. Through the centuries the unity of the Church has been present in the unity of her cult, her constitution, her doctrine. But even in her

---

2. Fideism: a belief in the incapacity of the intellect to attain knowledge of divine matters and a corresponding excessive emphasis on faith. (Tr. note.)

magisterium, her office to teach, the Church has often been hard pressed. In a phrase of Cardinal Newman's, she came at times close to a betrayal of the truth itself, and this through her highest custodians, appointed by our Lord Himself.

The situation is similar when we consider the holiness of the Church, stainless though she is in her substance. We know of the continuing sinfulness of even redeemed man. And if we Catholics continue to see the successor of Peter and the vicar of the crucified Christ even in a figure such as Alexander VI, let us confess that we reflect perhaps all too little on the shocking admission that is thereby implied. Therefore, let us have understanding for the subjective difficulties our Protestant brethren must feel in their consciences, formed as they are by the word of the Bible, on being confronted with our teachings. Let us first of all and emphatically admit: The unity of the Church is a mystery.

On the other side this, too, remains an inescapable conclusion: However one may interpret that unity which the Lord demands (John 17: 21), at the very least there cannot be any room for out and out contradictions. Churches or confessions or denominations which interpret the teachings of Christ in contradictory ways, are by their very contradictions incapable of representing the one body of the Lord in that unity which He demanded.

The exploration and continuing application of the doctrine which our Lord left to His Church, can never be completed. The Spirit of Truth promised by the Lord leads us on continually into all truth (John 16: 13).[3] The

3. John 16, 13: "But when he, the Spirit of truth has come, he will teach you all the truth. For he will not speak on his own authority, but

mysteries of God are many, and we can exhaust none of them.

The Lord Himself summed up the essential truth of His message of salvation in a few sentences (in the great commandment of love, in the Beatitudes, in the Our Father). The Church on her part adheres to this day to the twelve articles of the Creed in which she formulated the entire treasure of Revelation. But because it is God who speaks, the almighty giver of all life, a single *one* of His words suffices to reveal His truth to us in love. It is possible to say that the core of the whole doctrine is contained in every word of the Lord.

Of course, the divine truth does not reveal itself in every word of God with exactly the same intensity, substantiality, clarity, and immediacy. Because the Word became flesh, it partakes of the imperfections of created things; it permits of more than one meaning. If therefore we want to clarify fully the substance of the message of salvation from a specific word of the Scriptures, we shall have to protect it on all sides against misinterpretation; we must attempt to express its meaning as unequivocally as possible. Such clarity is necessary whenever we intend to speak with our separated brothers about the truth. If the problem we have here indicated is of concern to us, if our sinful self-righteousness urges us to claim a certain point of view of ours as in accordance with God's will, or if over the centuries the habit of a certain opinion has become like second nature to us, then we have to exercise special caution so that we do not, instead of seeking the will of God, merely profess our own.

---

whatever he will hear he will speak, and the things that are to come he will declare to you."

Now our subject here is the Reformation, more precisely, its genesis. Even in its beginnings it was more than just a collection of doctrines. It was an individually evolved general concept of Christianity and of its corresponding ecclesiastical form. Today it is something grown over the centuries, something that has become "second nature" to many of its adherents, endowed with an immense power of perseverance. Although the Protestant Churches are based on the theology and the theological principles of the Reformation, they also are vital activities of our own day; and neither their adherents nor their opponents can change them simply by means of logical or historical syllogisms, however well-founded.

On The Causes of the Christian Schism

Our first concern has been to establish a positive attitude in ourselves for the dialogue with our separated Christian brothers. Our endeavor is motivated by the realization that, in the words of our Lord, it is the unity or disunity of Christians which will decide whether or not His message will be a life-giving influence in the world. With this premise established, we now approach the specific question: How did the split come about? How was it possible? What are the causes of the Reformation? We must pose these questions and we must answer them not in order to arrive at an accounting, but in order to serve the will of the Lord, and also to resist properly the evil of disunity.

Whether or not we shall succeed in carrying on this conversation about the causes of the Reformation—or more exactly the schism—in the spirit of charity, depends mostly on us Catholics. For the Reformation is not only the action of the great reformers, Luther, Zwingli, or Calvin, it is also, and above all, the fruit of a long Catholic development.

In other words, the essential question here is not: What new doctrines did Luther or Calvin introduce, but: How was it possible that his renunciation of the old Church was accepted by so many, so that out of his personal theological teachings could arise the all-engulfing Reformation and with it the split, the schism?

That this was possible, is proof that there must have been a spiritual and intellectual disposition for such a rupture in the European Christian community of nations. When Luther and Calvin appeared on the scene, Western Christianity was to a considerable extent already ripe for a separation from the Roman Church, the Church of the popes—only nobody knew it. Even in those instances where Luther's and Calvin's teachings were presented in substantially polemic forms, in the beginning they appeared to most listeners not as something absolutely new, but merely as a continuation of the inner-ecclesiastic struggle which had been going on for centuries for the reform of the Church in its head and members.

This was all the more true as the polemic of the reformers arose from and centered on substantial Christian doctrines which were a widely shared, common Christian concern.

Our evangelical brethren have a right to emphasize this fact. On the other hand, even though the astonishing speed with which the teachings of the reformers spread is thus explained, the schism as such is thereby not justified.

We Catholics who regard the manner in which the

reformers formulated and presented those common Christian doctrines as a deviation from the Christian tradition, cannot be satisfied with the above explanation; for we also see in the consequences of the Reformation and in some of its tenets an erroneous development. This must be mentioned here so that we do not lose sight of the question of true unity in doctrine, dogmatic unity.

But let us return to the origins of the schism. About the year 1500 nobody could suspect, in spite of all prophecies of impending disaster, that an all-engulfing revolutionary change in the attitude of the European nations toward the traditional Church was in the making. Private and public life at the turn of that century was under the domination of papal, episcopal, and sacerdotal forms. We need to find an explanation how it was psychologically as well as judicially and economically possible that overnight, so to speak, a host of admirers of the monastic religious life became its worst enemies. The concepts of the Reformation grossly contradicted in most essentials the customs of thought and living of the preceding centuries; far beyond the circles of theologians and ecclesiastics they were realized as a clear break with papal authority which up to then had been considered as the indispensable condition for eternal salvation. Now suddenly this authority was being denounced as anti-Christian, as eternal corruption. Just how can it be explained that so many took part in this revolutionary turn? What changes in thinking, feeling, and believing had taken place?

However one tries to answer these questions, they all lead back to the Catholic past. Movements, thoughts, conditions, neglect within the Catholic sphere of life had caused those spiritual and intellectual shifts which triggered the coming of the Reformation and assured its success. Even before one assembles the individual facts, this conclusion is obvious. One can escape it only through the childishly naive or willfully blind notion that the Reformation was artificially created through malicious lies.

In the past, this opinion was heard frequently on the Catholic side, and from time to time there is still an occasional individual who, living in the past, tries to revive this discredited view. But revolutions such as the Reformation, especially when its central body of doctrine and philosophy develops such staying power as to carry it over more than 400 years, are not created; they can only be released (a process in which the cooperation and coresponsibility of the creative personalities involved is by no means precluded).

As soon as we understand this, however, we find ourselves confronted by the urgent need for a penetrating Catholic examination of conscience. And this is also our best guarantee that our dialogue with our separated brethren will not be one of strife but will proceed in fraternal charity. When we ask where our guilt lies, then we stand, at least as far as intent is concerned, in the kind of Christian spirit we can share with others, and we may have the hope that our dialogue will be blessed.

But this attitude, even though we admit it as correct and although we may already begin to feel secure in it, is so much exposed to the weight of old habits of thought as well as to the pressures of human egoism that it is well to give it further support.

In looking back at the Reformation, Catholic and Protestant Christians are both partisan, each for their own side. They are heirs to sharp, passionate, even hate-filled disagreements. We must make an effort to neutralize these formerly so bitter mutual aggressions. Unless there is proof to the contrary, we should both grant each other good faith and good will. After all, the position of the reformers, even though it developed into actual attack, as well as the Catholic defense which turned into counter-attack, was in principle concerned with the honor of God. In this intent, the reformers are of one mind with the guiding motive of St. Ignatius: Before all else the honor of God! In principle, the reformers did not aim for a division of the Church but for its purification. Although Luther separated himself from the Church—and under what deplorable circumstances!—it can be said with all possible emphasis that his inner, deeply religious development made him grow out of the Church without any original, premeditated intention. Sad to say that soon afterwards the language and actions on both sides by no means corresponded any longer to the goal of penitential purification. In accordance with the divine revelation of Christ, the honor of God—to the degree that it is in our keeping—depends on a twofold virtue: strict truth and love. Only where both are respected and realized, are the will of God and the law of Christ fulfilled.

And now we must state once more and without reservation that in the fight for truth, for the purity of the word, love often suffered. In the presence of the Holy Eucharist, bound together in one body through His, kneeling before the sacrament which He instituted out of "love to the end" (John 13: 1), we cannot but deplore the mediocrity, the hardened uncharitableness, the terrible lack of comprehension with which the struggle of our fathers for the reform of the Church in the sixteenth century was burdened.

To His love we must open ourselves so that, as far as lies in us, we may in the spirit of the Lord examine our past before our common Father in heaven, and in unison with our brothers confess our guilt. We could learn from the moving words of Pope John XXIII, so earnestly spoken: "Permit us to call you brothers." That is to say, the point is not to sit in judgment, to condemn, to look down in arrogance on others, or to assert a right. We seek only the Lord and the unity of His Church.

Of course, this does not release us from the necessity of having to make judgments and rejections. As has been said before, truth must have absolute primacy; one cannot limit it without betraying truth itself. This necessity is a burden which we must endure. But, again, truth, the life-giving truth to which we look in Christ and which He Himself is—the truth which is a matter of life and death— does not exist without love.

Defects in the Catholic Church Before the Reformation

It cannot be the task of this sketchy narrative to describe in detail the various factors by and through which the Reformation was prepared; the intellectual, spiritual, economic, and political events and changes which helped to make it possible.

It is necessary, however, that we deeply absorb in our consciousness the fact we have already established: What we are here dealing with are not merely a few isolated events; they are events which are deeply characteristic of the Catholic life of the Middle Ages. Nor are they phenomena which occurred immediately before the Reformation. The more one thinks the problem through, the more one is forced to ask this disquieting question: To what extent did essentials we consider typical of medieval piety conform to the full spirit of the Gospel? And to what extent did they depart from the Gospel? Was the indispensable core of Christian revelation, the theology of the cross, sufficiently recognized and realized in the various concrete details of medieval piety? How much of this revelation was covered over by other aspects such as ecclesiastic and papal power, even feats of personal piety? To what degree was the characteristic piety of the Middle Ages sacramental?

To see that these are genuine and not merely rhetorical questions, it should suffice to recall a few facts. The mass conversion of the Germanic tribes came after only a very summary introduction into the world of the Gospels. Germanic thinking, as exemplified in the principle "I give so that you will give," or more exactly "I perform so you will reward me" was never quite overcome. The barrier of the Latin language made it impossible for great parts of the Germanic peoples to comprehend the mystery of the Mass, and therein was rooted the fundamental separation of the laity (which was emphasized physically—and with what thorough effect—by a screen erected between the nave and the choir in the churches). All this we must keep before our eyes, for every one of these details had its influence on the whole development of Christianity in the Germanic lands.

The aspects enumerated here are not the whole story, of course. The point is not to discredit the glory of the faith of the Middle Ages, but to see the weak spots and the factors which can be proven to have had historically a weakening influence on unity.

Although it is useful to recall them, we do not have to limit ourselves to the laments, criticisms, and reform demands of Catholic bishops, theologians, and laymen loyal to the Church at the time just before the Reformation: the decades when the abuses in the Church were crying to heaven. Besides the flood of complaints from all countries, we have the moving confession of guilt of the personally blameless Pope Adrian VI (1522-1523), the official suggestions of the congregations especially appointed by Pope Paul III to prepare for reforms, the unrestrained accusations of the preachers at the Council of Trent, and finally the countless statements of synods throughout the second half of the sixteenth century.

To determine the historical role of the just-mentioned "abuses" in relation to the question we are asking, we must steer clear of wide-spread misunderstandings. What matters most are not in the main *moral* defects, whether in the Curia, in the higher or lower clergy, or in the monasteries. We must find a deeper meaning for the word "abuses," a meaning such as Bernard of Clairvaux gave it in his moving laments and indictments addressed to his former disciple Pope Eugene III. We shall hear more about these appeals later.

Certainly the moral laxity in the lives of the higher and lower clergy at the time of the Renaissance was a scandal without precedent. We do not intend to minimize these moral defects. The inner contradiction between the life of the clergy as it was practiced and the idea of the priesthood was so great that—speaking in purely natural terms—the concept of the priesthood itself could not help being damaged. For the clerical life as it was reflected by many of its representatives had deteriorated to an open violation of the Ten Commandments, not even to mention the spirit of perfection required by the Gospels. That un-Christian practices were widespread, even and especially in the highest office and in the center of Christianity, had a particularly demoralizing effect. Alexander VI as successor of St. Peter and vicar of the crucified Christ, or Leo X who looked at the papal office as a legitimate source of pleasure bestowed on him by God: the scandal of such men was not a minor blemish; it was a manifestation which, together with other acute forms of worldliness, represented the Church in such frivolity and contradiction to the spirit of the Gospel that one can understand that the words of such a hierarchy commanded little authority; it was powerless against a doctrine which pledged itself to forcing the Church and all Christendom back to the Cross.

The full significance of the ecclesiastical abuses of the Middle Ages, however, reveals itself in the *religious* sphere. One cannot help but see that the life and thinking of the clergy of that time, especially the hierarchy and the Curia, but also the money-collecting, often non-resident pastors and miserable "mass-readers," were prompted very little by prayer and sacrifice, by a priestly spirit, by a care for souls or for the training of new priests. How little their lives reflected the faith!

Yet, despite everything, these "abuses" were by no means the direct causes of the Reformation. With the great reformers the early beginnings are positive throughout, although they of course took liberal advantage of the existing wrongs and—sad to say—did not hesitate to exaggerate them. There is no doubt, however, that the abuses which did exist contributed to the weakening and finally to the disintegration of the Church's unity, and that Christians, having become distrustful and lukewarm, listened with mounting willingness to the words of the new preachers.

At the end of every discussion of the abuses, therefore, follows the realization that these things are dangerous not only as things evil in themselves but above all because they lead many to the conviction that a Church thus defiled could not possibly be the unblemished bride of the Lord. Long before the majority of the people consciously came to this conclusion, the Church had lost its attractiveness for them. The inner bonds that united them with the Church had more or less dissolved. That many did not notice it for so long only made the situation more hopeless.

One begins to comprehend fully the debilitating effect of this situation, when one realizes that the excesses are not mere isolated, accidental cases of human failings but are connected to certain structural characteristics of the medieval mixture of ecclesiastical and secular affairs; so intermingled were these in fact that the entire hierarchy would have had to be composed of saints for the progressive deterioration here sketched to have been arrested and obviated in the end. Consequently, the excesses were not really overcome until the historical circumstances of the medieval ecclesiastic structure had been eliminated or purified.

Thus, if we want to understand in some measure how it came about that the European nations so largely turned away from the papal Church, we must reach far back into the Middle Ages—back to that magnificent event which is universally recognized as a cleansing and renewal of the Church: the Gregorian reform. After its heroic period, however, this reform deviated perilously from its high ideal. In the first part of the twelfth century it was St. Bernard of Clairvaux, Doctor of the Church and reformer of the Benedictines of Cluny, who warned Pope Eugene III with prophetic force and admirable candor about the dangers and abuses that had arisen from a partial betrayal of the Gregorian reform, not the least of these abuses being the worldliness that emanated from the Roman Curia operating as a secular "court."

Bernard, personally a great supporter of the papacy in that century, fully acknowledges and praises the institution of a universal papacy as founded by Jesus, but basing his thought on the law of Christ, he sharply distinguishes in this religious and prophetic priestly office that which came into being as a result of Constantinian tradition and that which came in due to the Justinian concept of law. Even where the exterior power and wealth of a pope are legitimate, he notes soberly, *these* do not come from Peter. For "since Peter did not possess them, he could not hand them down."

Bernard's book *On Contemplation,* which he addressed to the pope, has been praised throughout the centuries as a guide for popes. When we read his thoughts and speak of "abuses" in his spirit, our judgment will be reliable and our examination of conscience in line with the true spirit of the Church.

In Bernard of Clairvaux we find both ecclesiastical loyalty and freedom such as are seldom encountered any more. We must listen to his fearless voice. In variation after variation, he places before the pope the singular nature of his universal office: Service, not domination!

Concern and labor, not splendor and wealth; the latter are not apostolic! Not Lord but steward! The pope is not allowed merely to follow his own will or, even worse, his whim; he must have a well-founded justification for his decisions. For not everything that is licit is proper, and other things can do harm where they should be helpful. Papal power is not a personal property but is given as a trust to its holder, otherwise the pope would usurp the power of God. By the same token, the pope is a judge only in things spiritual, not in things of the world. Everything, even the fullness of his power, must be directed to the care of souls.

Often Bernard criticizes overcentralization. The Roman Catholic Church is the mother of all Churches, not their lord. The pope is the shepherd of the entire flock including its shepherds; however, he is not the master of the bishops, but one of them. For beside the pope there are others who also open the gates of heaven, who have a flock of their own entrusted to them. There are various degrees to the hierarchy; if the pope usurps the functions of those below him, he erects a monstrosity. This daily overburdening of the pope requires him to sit in judgment on the application of laws—those of Justinian instead of those of the Lord. When will he have time to pray, to teach the nations—which he is not doing adequately (the mission to the pagans)—or to build up the Church?

What the pope is, he is by the grace of God. By himself, like all men, he is nothing. What he has of himself is evil; what is good in him, he has from the Lord. Certainly, "there is nothing more precious than a good and useful shepherd, but that is a rare bird."

Sad to say, what Bernard criticized in the system was

not changed. In spite of the great reform efforts (and successes) of Innocence III and of great saints and zealous reformers in both the secular and the monastic clergy, much evil continued to grow, past the time of Boniface VIII; these conditions led to the fiscal benefice system of Avignon and its heir: the Great Schism. Power became the aim of curial activity, as the Curia became increasingly enmeshed in politics and economic considerations. Under the benefice system, an ecclesiastical office was more and more looked upon as a source of income. Simony became one of the great evils. Pleasure-seeking in various forms stamped the life of the higher clergy. Devotional practices multiplied, but more for the "merit" to be gained than as expressions of a solid faith.

In some ways popular piety was extraordinarily deep and rich. Literature in the manner of *The Imitation of Christ* was widely disseminated and there existed an intense, truly spiritual Christian art. Even in the fad of making pilgrimages to the relics of saints one must not overlook the genuine sacrificial spirit of the faithful.

Yet even in this piety the true evangelical spirit is often covered up by grossly materialistic external elements. In the indulgence agreement between Pope Leo X and Archbishop Albrecht of Brandenburg-Mainz, which entailed the sale of indulgences by the latter's agent, Tetzel, we have an example of a revolting traffic in spiritual graces that inevitably aroused violent protest.

The Vagueness of Late-Medieval Theology

The Catholic of today asks with good reason how it was possible for Luther, who had grown up in the Church, to be a zealous and highly educated monk and yet misrepresent the doctrine of the Church to the extent that he actually did.

The answer is this: The Catholic of today thinks, as is easily understandable, of the situation created by the Council of Trent and the Vatican Council, where a great number of questions of faith were officially clarified and fundamental abuses were eliminated, and in part positively overcome.

No such clarity existed at the time in which Luther grew up. True, the pre-Reformation Church preserved in its official teaching, in its liturgy, and also somewhat in the teaching of Thomas Aquinas and other great theologians, the pure doctrine of Holy Scripture as we learn and teach it today; but the general intellectual situation of the time was not characterized by the clarity of these sources. What was really characteristic of the time was rather a *theological vagueness* which shows most obviously in the competition between the various theological schools, culminating in the nominalist thinking of the Franciscan William of Ockham (or Occam), who died in 1349. This thinking differs sharply not only from pre-scholastic theology but also from high scholasticism and even the substance of the liturgy.

The *fact of theological vagueness* can be shown from an abundance of proofs. This vagueness does not mean that the individual theologians were imprecise in their thinking; it does mean that various and even contradictory theological interpretations of the faith, even mutually exclusive fundamental theological concepts, were simultaneously represented in the Church, and not clearly separated as to truth and error. To this must be added that nominalism neglected some fundamental aspects of the

Gospels by means of highly arbitrary, even though skilful constructions.

In Occam's nominalism, for example, grace is actually not important at all, since it is reduced to a caprice of God who could just as well have required lecherousness and theft for eternal life as chastity and honesty. There were also theologians who taught that man could gain eternal life through his own natural powers.

Opinions on the primacy of the pope were by no means uniform. This primacy was unrestrainedly exaggerated by some, belittled as much as possible by others. Some held a democratic, quantitative concept of the Church, that is to say, a church without the sacramental conception of total creative existence, in being before any of its members and more than the sum of all of them.

Practical theology, as it existed in the curias of the popes and bishops or was being preached from the pulpits, blended this inorganic theological mixture into a product which often was far removed from the strength of the Gospel and its inner spirit, its theology of the Cross.

The reality of this theological vagueness can be hardly imagined by Catholics of our day. But the unprejudiced reader of the sources can see it for himself, in all its astounding detail, in the long drawn-out disputations that preceded the formulation of dogmas at the Council of Trent. The Council spoke quite candidly about the existing "confusio opiniorum," the mass of conflicting opinions in evidence there.

The logical vagueness was of special importance in relation to the Eucharist and the Mass. Here, too, we stumble into a sea of confusion.

Thomas Aquinas had explained the Eucharist of the

Mass in close relation with the passion and death of the Lord as both a symbol and a means of unity within the Church, the one body of Christ. Before the Reformation, however, the doctrine of the Eucharist had shrunk to a strictly private devotion based only on faith in the real presence of the Lord in the eucharistic bread.

This doctrine fared even worse with Occam and his heirs. The Occamism of the fifteenth century—e.g., Gabriel Biel's explanation of the Canon of the Mass (the main work for Luther's formation)—cannot be equated with what Occam himself taught, but Occam cannot be simply eliminated from the development of Luther.

Although Occam wrote two tracts on the Eucharist, his only real interest in this central religious mystery is a logical one, namely, whether in the consecrated host quality and quantity fall into one. Luther judges correctly when he summarizes his impression of these works (even though exaggerating as he is wont to do) in the words: "What others have found there [in this philosophic theology] I do not know; I only know that it was there that I lost Christ."

Luther remained deeply affected by the Occamists' atomistic method of thinking. Although he steadily adheres to an acknowledgment of sacraments, in essence he does not think sacramentally. For this reason, his concept of the Church is strangely weak: the Church is not seen as the sacramental womb bringing forth the individual faithful as a member of one body, but merely as the sum of the believers.

The theology of some of Luther's adversaries, however, was not an expression of sacramental thinking either. This is the case with the zealous Dr. Johann Eck, who knew Scripture inside out, but did not substantially think in its spirit. He amasses as many school proofs as possible to document the sacrificial character of the Mass but is incapable of illuminating the position theologically; that is to say, from the nature of the faith. In the face of such pedantry Luther could without presumption hold to his opinion that it was he who remained more literally true to the word of God.

Although the Church had other, more fruitful methods to represent its concept of the Eucharist and the Mass, these were not widely used in the controversy with Luther. The Catholic Mass practice of the time must bear much of the blame for this neglect. We must remember that throughout the Middle Ages the doctrine of the sacrament of the altar and of the Mass had not been understood very profoundly by the people and their priests. The circles in which people prayed and partook of Holy Communion, as the fourth book of the *Imitation of Christ* shows, were rather few. More significant (and religiously more dangerous) was the shameful and widespread practice of "reading" Masses apart from a liturgical context for the "fruits" they were calculated to produce.

What can we do today regarding this question? We must become aware of the truth that the simple and solemn words of the institution of the Eucharist are something we have in common with our separated brethren through the language of the synoptics and of Paul who, in their naive way, mean no more than they say. The words of Paul on the sacrament of the body and blood of Jesus, as Paul preaches the death of the Lord, and the report of the synoptics on the events that prepared for and surrounded the passion of our Lord, contain all the elements necessary for an understanding of the communal celebration of the Eucharist as a sacrifice of redemption. That there is only *one* redemptive sacrifice, is something we no longer feud about. The Mass is only a *representation* of this one, unrepeatable sacrifice. The Council of Trent says so. We repeat it. We must confess that Catholic thought has not always adequately interpreted this dogma, but we are now moving away from our past mistakes.

Remembering that the formulation of a dogma does not amount to the canonization of a school of thought, we can apply what has been said above to Catholic teaching on transubstantiation. This dogma is not rooted in the Aristotelian concept of *substantia*, but in the reality which the word means to describe: that which is, the *essence* of a thing. The dogma of transubstantiation says that a change takes place in the elements of bread and wine in such a way that after the consecration the body and blood of the Lord are essentially, really, and truly present. That no change takes place visually and in taste, is evident. This we, as well as our separated brethren, can profess as our belief.

The Great Papal Schism

It cannot be doubted that in the sixteenth century Church and faith were split in the full meaning of the word only after the Reformation and in consequence of it. Despite the tragic divisions in earlier Christianity already mentioned (some of which had world-wide effects), the real rupture in Christianity dates only from the sixteenth century. Because the Reformation brought about a partially new concept of Christianity, the split has since widened and deepened. This fundamentally new concept, which rent the unity of Christian belief, is both climaxed and rooted in the rejection of the teaching authority of the pope and in the sacramental hierarchy, that is to say, the sacramental priesthood. In short, what is involved is a different concept of the Church.

But even this assault against the unity of the Church had been prepared by Catholics themselves. The insubordinate and reckless criticism poured forth for centuries by theologians, canonists, statesmen, and princes against the papacy, against the orthodoxy of either the Roman or the Avignon Church, a criticism levelled in all possible forms, not even shrinking from the accusation of heresy —all this had amounted to a thorough preparatory job for a definite break.

Already at the beginning of the fourteenth century, theses of such radicalism were circulated against the nature of the Church and the power of the pope that they would hardly be outdone by the proposals of the sixteenth century. The spectacle of numerous anti-popes, put in office through power politics rather than for religious reasons, and the various small schisms created thereby throughout the Middle Ages, had long before the Reformation either gravely damaged the unity of the Church or caused it to appear as something merely extraneous that did not really matter.

Finally the great Western Schism had come upon the Church as the direct fruit of ecclesiastical politics and the finance-orientated thinking of the cardinals and some of the popes. This schism lasted from 1378 to 1417 (or rather 1449, when the last anti-pope of the Great Schism resigned, only a few years before Luther's birth). These were the four decades during which there were always two, sometimes even three, reigning popes, each with his own curia of cardinals, and each excommunicating the other as heretical, along with the faithful who adhered to him. So confused had the situation become that it was practically impossible to determine who the legitimate pope was and where the legitimate Church was. Saints were on the side of the Avignon as well as the Roman popes. The division permeated all countries, ecclesiastical provinces and orders, and numerous monasteries and parishes. And because of the economic burdens and the feuds over church benefices engendered by this division, it came to be a profound experience of internal dissension and of ecclesiastical uncertainty; it so penetrated all levels of the then existing nations that the West could not easily forget it. From this prolonged, unprecedented state of disarray stemmed the great strength of the new conciliar theory which wanted to make Church councils (especially the one in Basel) into parliaments, and the Church into a kind of democracy. It was a moment of great peril for the Church.

Luther's fight against the primacy of the pope must be seen against the background of these conditions. His thesis went much further than those of his predecessors, but many believed (especially in the beginning of the Reformation) that in his words they heard only what they had heard before—something long disputed in the Church, but not something revolutionary or impossible.

If we consider the theological vagueness together with the weakened Christian unity, and if we consider how little power of conviction the word of the Church, laden with abuses as she was, could command, we must admit that at the end of the Middle Ages it was relatively easy for someone with a theologically independent mind to become a heretic, especially if such a man was moved in heart and soul by the central religious idea of Christianity.

The several symptoms of feebleness we have briefly reviewed acted together as an organic force; they grew together and produced a state of religious anemia, a critical spiritual-ecclesiastical consumption. And let us not forget that the general disorder and uncertainty afforded the best possible atmosphere for the development of dangerous partisan passions.

Surveying these severe symptoms of ecclesiastical weakness and the Christian disloyalty in many areas, one cannot but be moved, even shaken, by this terrible decline, this inner decay which could no longer be balanced in practice by the theory of the purity of the Church's doctrine and the holiness of the Church's substance. One can readily see that it was easy for a revolt to get started in an institution whose pure ideal had been betrayed in so many instances by its own leaders. When the revolt came, it actually seemed justified by the feebleness of the body attacked; besides, there simply was not enough strength left in the body to summon sufficient powers of resistance.

For us today, this is the main realization: The causes that made the Reformation possible and which typify certain general conditions in the pre-Reformation Church are Catholic causes; more correctly, they developed during a Catholic period, in a Catholic place; they demanded a radical removal because they amounted to a curtailment of the Catholic substance itself.

And therefore it is true that the Reformation was prepared to a shocking degree by Catholic failures. To that extent it has Catholic causes and—speaking in Christian terms—there is Catholic guilt. An express and specific Catholic *mea culpa* is in order.

Luther's Concerns and Luther's Opponents

In a Catholic examination of conscience we must naturally include the question: Did our fathers take note with sufficient openmindedness of the religious concerns for which the reformers labored?

As far as Luther is concerned, one has to allow in fairness to the Church that in many cases he made it extraordinarily difficult for her to hear him out attentively. The rude force of Luther's polemic, together with his revolutionary condemnation of practically the entire system by which the Church lived—the pope, the sacramental hierarchy, monasticism, and the Mass—made it difficult from the beginning and increasingly so as time progressed, to recognize and scrutinize justifiable complaints in his massive attacks and distortions. It was an assault that threatened the very existence of the Church. In many instances, Luther made such obviously outrageous misrepresentations of fundamental Catholic teachings and the motivations of the spiritual life that it remains a riddle to this day how he could have gone so far and how it was possible that so many others, who had grown up in the Church, could agree with his exaggerations. Here is a field where careful and scholarly research is still needed. Protestant colleagues should help us in this work with much greater personal independence than has been the case thus far.

But an explanation is not a justification. What is often lacking on the Catholic side is the simple willingness to listen. This sin of omission is observable with relatively few exceptions in the Catholic theological positions through the entire history of the Reformation.

The Lutheran, Zwinglian, and Calvinist reforms were not only apostasy and heresy. How little impression have Luther's first theses on indulgences made on the Catholic side: "When our Lord and Master Jesus Christ said, Do penance, He wanted the entire life of the faithful to be penitential." How foolish it was of the zealous Dr. Eck to try to prove this un-Catholic!

How impossibly blind were all those many Catholic theologians who would not see that Luther's "justification through faith," is thoroughly Catholic in its central concern.

It is therefore all the more redeeming that, in the words of the extraordinarily understanding Cardinal Gasparo Contarini, the main accomplishment of the Council of Trent, which condemned Luther, was the decree on justification. We know today that in the doctrine of justification, the point on which Luther thought his case would stand or fall, our thinking is essentially identical with his and that of Calvin. True, the fathers of the Council of Trent had to struggle for a long time before they agreed on the final formula, but they did pronounce that *nothing* productive of salvation is possible without grace, without faith; and they added that even our merits are gifts from God.

Today we are finally beginning to see that on this

decisive point we have misunderstood each other for four hundred years.

We are drawing together in a similar way in our understanding of the Eucharist and of the Mass as a sacrifice. In the words of the Council of Trent, the Lord Jesus Christ Himself is the One who is immolating and is immolated— the priest is only the instrument. A further belief we discovered we have in common is the problem of Gospel and law, judged of central importance by the reformers.

It is worthy of note that these discoveries of things we have in common are not isolated events. They stem from a "new" Catholic way of theological thinking which is endeavoring to base its categories as much as possible on Holy Scripture. In the process, the dried-up scholastic formulas become rich again and can immediately be carried over from the area of theology to the area of prayer.

Thus in re-evaluating the monastic theology of St. Bernard, we rediscover the Catholic substance in formulas which for a long time have appeared heretical to us, e.g., the rightly understood phrase "sola scriptura" which is found in Bernard and Thomas Aquinas, the interrelation of "continuing sin" and transforming justification in man; we recognize more profoundly that the infusion of created grace is a personal, living act which God performs in man.

We know of course, (1) that in some of the utterances of the reformers these doctrines were so presented as though they were excluding other truths, a one-sidedness which did not do justice to the fullness of all the scriptural affirmations; and (2) that up to this day there exist well-nigh insuperable differences in our concepts of the Church and especially in the interpretation of the Church's teaching authority. But that changes nothing in those central things we do have in common. However, it is necessary that the fact of our common spiritual possessions penetrate much more deeply into the Catholic as well as the Protestant consciousness, if the work of pacification is to be advanced. After all, where should the possibility of a mutual understanding be more evident than here?

But once we recognize that there is much that we deeply hold in common through our faith in the one Lord in whose name we are baptized, there will grow from this faith the resolve to study the Reformation and its causes, and with this resolve the readiness to admit our Catholic failures and our guilt.

A Catholic Confiteor

Having arrived thus far, our eyes are opened also to the blessing that flows from our own confession of guilt. To begin with, we have of course not even the right to ask what this will profit us. For, apart from our commitment to the truth, the Alpha and Omega of the Gospels is penance; the essential requirement of *metanoia* stands, like everything else, under the word: "Thy will be done." We have not even the right to ask for assurances against a possible exploitation of our admission of guilt. Besides, we are no longer in the political sphere. At the time of the Reformation, the Confiteor of Adrian VI could be misused by his enemies in the realm of both secular and Church politics. This danger does not exist any more today.

On the contrary, the more each side confesses its guilt, the more charity grows, and the search for truth with it.

It can be affirmed that the Catholic position has been considerably strengthened by our "mea culpa." This sincere "mea culpa" has opened the hearts of many of our separated brothers and has furthered the general aspiration for unity.

In the spirit of our mutual "mea culpa" our separated brothers now can—despite the obstacles that still remain—kneel down together with us, and together with us adore the one Lord. As far as is in our power, we should hold open this possibility for them.

Are the Reformers to Blame?

It would be unhistorical, unrealistic, and un-Christian not to include in our examination of conscience our attitudes toward the fathers of the Reformation. The principle to keep in mind is precisely that formulated by Otto Karrer recently: *"Either all are responsible or nobody is."* This is not to say that the guilt is the same on both sides. But let it emphatically be repeated: We do not intend to let the spirit of contention and of an arrogant sitting-in-judgment enter in through another door here. It is exactly at this point that we must remember the admonition of Pope John XXIII: "We shall not attempt to settle accounts with each other."

We are one with our Protestant brothers in the resolve that truth must have primacy. And the truth, even when tempered with charity, can be hard and bitter.

But even in this context there are possibilities for a meeting of minds. For, although we are engaged in searching out the responsibility of the reformers, we want to remain fully objective. None but God knows how, in the final judgment, a man stands before Him. And into this knowledge of the King we have no intention of intruding with our brashness.

The fact that objective truth and an individual's subjective profession of the truth often vary, and the other fact that even in a man of good will the decisions of his conscience do change often—these are fundamental phenomena in the history of man. In the face of this reality, it requires some audacity to maintain that defection from the faith without personal guilt is impossible.

In recent times it has been stated repeatedly that the capability of man to believe on faith has been diminished. Reasons for this phenomenon have been shown for which countless masses of victims simply cannot be held responsible; yet these were reasons which caused them to fall away from the perhaps already weak faith into which they were born. The conclusion has been drawn that the possibility of apostasy without guilt is increasing in our world.

Now, one of the facts of the pre-Reformation period, which crystalizes more clearly with the increasing analysis of available sources, is the one stated above: The religious-ecclesiastical and theological situation was such that it was easy for anyone with a theologically independent mind to become a heretic. Hardly anything can be proven with greater clarity in the genesis of the Reformation, in the defection of Luther as well as of Calvin and of many other first-generation leaders of the Reformation than this: They did not leave the Church with premeditation. They had not intended originally to separate themselves from her.

On the other hand Luther had been born into the Catholic faith and had been raised in it. He was a Catholic priest and monk. And then he lost confidence in the Church. Could this have happened if the whole of the Gospel had not been diminished in some degree for him? Brother Schütz of the Protestant monastic community of Taizé hints at this when he asks: "Do we [Protestants] still possess all the dimensions of the truth if we exclude the long tradition of the first sixteen centuries?"

The principle here, seems clear: If God spoke, if He appeared in the flesh and founded a Church with the commission to teach—as Luther also believed—then only to that Church and its teaching office is His truth entrusted. No individual can claim the right to interpret this truth in any other way than the Church does. Luther himself gave expression to this truth in his early discourses, and it still weighs on our hearts.

And therefore, with all we have said, with all our respect for the good intentions of the reformers, our question remains unanswered, and the Protestant examination of conscience is not finished. In Luther's sincere and deeply moving pleading for a merciful God are many deficiencies, and in his tremendous work as reformer and preacher the mistakes are quite obvious.

Luther did not fully hear the Church, and he who so absolutely wanted to put himself under the judgment of the Word, was not fully a hearer of the Word.

This is not the place to go into this aspect any further. It is a chapter by itself; and even if fully completed, it does not eliminate Luther's fundamental intent. He cried out to God for mercy, and he wanted to prevent any diminution of the glory of God in favor of men. Unfortunately, to desire something is not the same as to achieve it.

To repeat: If we want to speak fruitfully about the unity to be regained, love must be at work in us—love of the Lord, love of His Church, love of the brethren: "Truth in charity"—charity bears all. Love was the compelling motive of Him who was sent specifically to the sinners and to those in error. I am not permitted to love what is unholy in me and in the Church; neither am I permitted to love whatever is error in my separated brother. But I must love him who is separated from me, as he is, insofar as he is not consciously opposed to the will of God. In dialogue with one separated from me, I must imitate Him who was sent to me, the sinner—and to him, the sinner.

And then there is the other fundamental fact: Although only in the Church is there salvation, it is also the teaching of the Church that the saving grace and truth of God is not confined within the limits of the visible form of the Church. Therefore, I too must stand in love and in respect before whatever God has wrought in faith, in hope, in charity outside the visible Catholic Church. And herein belong first of all our separated *Christian* brethren. Together with them we must pray:

Thy Kingdom Come.

2

WILHELM DE VRIES, SJ | # THE EASTERN CHURCH AND CHRISTIAN UNITY

UNITY OF ALL Christians in the one true Church of Jesus Christ—this is the longing of the entire Christian world today. However, there are great obstacles on the road that would lead to the realization of this end. Paradoxical as it may sound, the greatest obstacle is the kind of unification already achieved down to the last detail within the Catholic Church of the West. More accurately expressed, it is not so much this unification as such, which may indeed be right for the Church of an essentially homogeneous cultural sphere, but the particular idea of a world-wide Church unity which we have fashioned for ourselves, based exclusively on the realities of Western Catholicism, which now constitutes an obstacle. We used to praise, for example, the ideal of a uniform Mass for the entire Church, even sung, if possible, to the same choral melody. Or we spoke, as a matter of course, of Latin as *the* language of the Catholic Church. When confronted with the obvious objection that there are, after all, within the Catholic Church Eastern liturgies with their own languages, we retreat with the excuse that our reference was of course only to the *Latin* Church.

But for us to speak matter-of-factly of the *whole*

51

Church without taking cognizance of the diversities which actually do exist within the true universal Church, indicates that we are lacking in the true appreciation of our truly catholic breadth, and that we have not acquired a consciousness of the fact that the world-embracing Church must provide room for the polymorphic variety and multicolored diversity of all the peoples who are to find in this Church their spiritual home.

An eminent representative of the Catholic Church of the East, the Patriarch Maximos IV of Antioch, Jerusalem, and Alexandria, formulated this truth not long ago in a conversation with the former Lord Mayor of Florence, Giorgio La Pira, in a perhaps somewhat provocative manner, when he said: "One would have to begin by converting the Latin West to Catholicism, namely to the universality of the teaching of Christ . . . Casting every one into the same mold is incompatible with Catholic universality." What? Are we in the West not truly Catholic? Certainly we are. But we are in danger of creating for ourselves an image of Church unity which is irreconcilable with catholicity. This is *the* greatest obstacle to the reunion of all Christians.

There are many Christians who for centuries have gone their own ways, have developed their own distinct forms of public worship, have evolved their own religious traditions, and have translated and transplanted the Christian truth into the languages of their own spiritual and intellectual worlds. If we want to force on these Christians our own Western Catholicism as we have developed it with all the minutiae of music, incense, shape and color of liturgical vestments and so on, as though these were the only right and acceptable forms, then we are barring for them the way to God's true Church which is necessary for salvation; then we may perhaps be more or less able to make individual converts to the Catholic Church, but we shall have to forget about winning entire separated communities for reunion.

We should instead look to what is essential for the unity of the Church—to that on which all who want to belong to Christ's Church *must* agree, as compared to what is only accidental or ornamental.

A good look at the Catholic Church of the East, which has preserved its own specific rites and traditions, its hierarchical structure, its form of piety and also its characteristic theology, may bring us closer to an understanding of this problem. Once we logically think through the principles which underlie the recognition of an autonomous Eastern Church within the framework of the universal Church, unthought-of perspectives open up for an organic union of all separated Christians within the one true Church of Jesus Christ.

Whenever in the course of the centuries efforts were made to win the separated Churches of the East to reunion with Rome, popes and councils have clearly pronounced what is necessary to achieve such a union. Pius IX, for example, in his Letter *In Suprema Petri Apostoli Sede* of January 6, 1848, inviting the separated patriarchs and bishops of the East to reunion, wrote these words:

> We do not impose any burden on you except that which is necessary, namely that, having returned to union, you agree with us in the profession of the true faith which the Catholic Church holds and teaches, and that you

maintain communion with the Church itself
and its Supreme Chair of Peter. As far as your
sacred rites are concerned, only those would
have to be disallowed which somehow would
be counter to the faith and to Catholic unity,
and which might have crept in during the
time of separation. [1]

In a similar vein spoke Pope John XXIII about that
which is necessary for the unity of the Church in his first
encyclical *Ad Petri Cathedram,* dated June 26, 1959. He
affectionately invited the "brothers and sons" separated
from the Apostolic See into their ancient home, their
Father's house, which is not anything strange to them:

We beg of you to understand well that our
loving appeal to Church unity does not invite
you to come into a strange home, but into our
common house, the house of the Father. Permit us to exhort you, whom we love tenderly
in the heart of Jesus Christ (Phil. 1: 8) that
you remember your fathers who preached the
word of God to you. Contemplate the happy
issue of the life they lived and imitate their
faith (Hebr. 13: 7).

In his Christmas message of 1958 Pope John had already
spoken of this house which is familiar to the separated
brethren "because their fathers also illuminated it once
with their sublime doctrine and adorned it with their
virtues." What they must accept in this house in order to

---

1. R. De Martinis, *Juris Pontifici de Propaganda Fide,* Vol. VI, 1,
Rome, 1894, pp. 52–53.

become again sons of equal right, is only the absolutely necessary things, not the accessories, ornaments, and decorations which the brothers who stayed home have, according to their taste, accumulated over the centuries.

These necessary things, said the Pope, are the *one faith, unity in guidance,* and *the same cult.*

Divine revelation must be accepted in substance and without reservation by anyone who wants to be a Catholic. This, however, as the Pope specifically emphasized, is quite compatible with a healthy freedom of discussion on unsettled questions. Said the Pope:

> There are, however, various aspects on which the Catholic Church leaves freedom of discussion to the theologians, to the extent that such matters are not yet clarified and that such discussions will not injure the unity of the Church but on the contrary will lead to a better and more profound insight into the dogmas concerned and will bring to light new aspects revealed by the confrontation of opinions.

The guiding principle shall be: "Unity in that which is necessary, freedom in that which is in doubt, but in everything charity."

Unity in guidance consists of the subordination of the faithful under the priests, the priests under the bishops, and the bishops under the pope as the successor of Peter (in matters of faith and morals and legitimate ecclesiastical jurisdiction).

Unity in cult is essentially established through the Holy Sacrifice of the Mass and the seven sacraments.

The pope did *not* speak, however, of uniformity of rites and liturgical traditions. Uniformity is not needed. Indeed, Pope John expressly recognized diversity in rites. Said he:

> This does not preclude the well-known fact that there are within the Catholic Church various legitimate rites which only increase the luster of its beauty: "All glorious is the King's daughter . . . in embroidered apparel" (Ps. 44: 15).

Let us now see in detail how the essential unity of cult, guidance, and doctrine is understood by the Church.

To begin with the least difficult: Unity of cult.

It is a matter of course today that the Catholic Church wants to see the Eastern rites preserved. It accepts these rites not reluctantly or merely because the Eastern Christians, who are strongly attached to their time-honored liturgical forms, cannot be won over in any other way for reunion. The Catholic Church accepts these rites with full conviction and in the realization that the variety of nationalities which belong to the world-wide Church, practically requires a multiplicity of rites and liturgical traditions; that this diversity is therefore not a necessary evil merely to be tolerated, but a genuine value; that uniformity would not be an ideal, but would do violence to life itself which must evolve in various forms according to its own inherent laws.

The great pope of union, Leo XIII, in his Apostolic Letter *Orientalium Dignitas*, of November 30, 1894, termed the variety of Eastern rites the best evidence for the catholicity of the Church and simultaneously for its properly understood unity. He wrote:

> The preservation of the Oriental rites is much more important than anyone would think. The venerable age that distinguishes the various forms of these rites is an adornment for the entire Church while at the same time it permits the divine unity of the Catholic faith to be made manifest. From this flows the proof, on the one side, for the apostolic origin of the most important Churches of the East, and from this rises their ancient and intimate union with the Roman See. There is perhaps no more miraculous evidence for the catholicity of God's Church than this unique adornment lent to her by the various forms of ceremonies and the ancient, venerable languages which are all the more noble because they are derived from the Apostles and the Fathers. Thus, the unique homage which was rendered to the newly-born Christ by the Wise Men from the East who came to adore him is, as it were, continually being renewed.[2]

Pope Pius XI also expressed this thought in his Moto Proprio *Sanctae Dei Ecclesiae,* of March 3, 1938:

> While some individuals, out of an exaggerated zeal for unity and for want of familiarity with the Orientals and their individualities, may have attempted at times to change their sacred rites and make them over to resemble

---

2. Leonis XIII, *Pontificis Maximi Acta,* Vol. XIII, Rome, 1894, pp. 360–361.

the Latin rite, the Roman popes, our predecessors, have resisted such attempts as best as
they could and with all the means at their
command. . . . For the Roman popes are of the
opinion that a diversity in things liturgical
which is based on the characteristics of the
various nationalities is not only not contrary
to the holy faith and the unity of the divine
service, it actually puts this unity into the
proper light.[3]

Pope Pius XII dwelled on similar thoughts in his first
encyclical, *Summi Pontificatus:*

The Church of Jesus Christ, as the faithful
guardian of the exalted Divine wisdom, does
not intend to minimize in any way the characteristic individualities of the various nationalities which these people rightly hold in
honor as their sacred tradition. What the
Church desires is a union born of the charity
which is to bind all together, but not merely
for the sake of an exterior egalitarianism
which would only weaken interior strength.[4]

The diversity in liturgical matters which developed in
the East, in direct contrast to the West, has its historical
foundation in the cultural multiplicity of the Orient.
There, the Hellenistic bent of mind, widespread though
it was everywhere else, could not simply displace the
other, more ancient cultures. Thus it came about that the

3. *Acta Apostol. Sedis,* XXX, 1938, pp. 154–155.
4. *Acta Apostol. Sedis,* XXXL, 1939, p. 428.

various peoples of the East, Greeks, Syrians, Egyptians, Ethiopians, Armenians, created out of their own characteristic cultures and languages those special liturgical forms for the Holy Sacrifice and for the dispensation of the sacraments which were suited to their particular genius. The Church has always accepted this diversity and where schism was overcome, it granted to those who returned to ecclesiastical unity with Rome the privilege to retain their traditional rites, as long as the one faith and the essential oneness of the cult in the Holy Sacrifice and the seven sacraments was preserved.

In the West, Rome, acting as a dominant center and seat of the successor of Peter, imposed the Western cultural pattern, born out of Latin Christianity, on the Germanic tribes that were converted. Constantinople, on the other hand, which attempted to create a similar unity in the East, showed a much greater willingness to adapt itself to existing cultural patterns, specifically in the sphere of liturgical languages. Who knows whether the rebellion of the greater part of the Germanic nations against Rome had not as at least one reason the all too strict uniformity in liturgical matters that had been imposed on them?

At any rate, these Eastern nations, in the course of their separation from Rome, have produced liturgical forms of their own in the language of their people. Can all this simply be put aside if a great corporate reunion of these separated communities with Rome is to be made possible? Once the right conclusions are drawn from the realization that diversity in liturgical matters is rooted in the individual characteristics of different peoples, the way will have been opened that will make possible the recognition of such forms which have sprung from the soil of these peoples and which are peculiarly suited to them—even though they have grown outside the Catholic Church. Of course, these liturgies would have to be adapted to the Catholic faith; the Holy Sacrifice and the seven sacraments would have to be incorporated, for they belong to the essential unity in cult which the Church cannot relinquish.

For the Catholics of the East, the Catholic Church also recognizes the individuality of their traditions, including the tradition of a married clergy. There is no valid reason why a similar accommodation should not also be possible with respect to Western communities willing to join the unity of the Church.

The second point: How is the essential unity in guidance understood by the Church?

In order to find an answer to this question, we must again look to the attitude of the Church toward the Christian East, the validity of whose own hierarchical structure is recognized by Rome. In the Western ecclesiastical constitution, the intermediate steps that existed in the early Church between the supreme authority of the pope and the authority of the individual local bishops, have been omitted. In this situation the danger may arise that the doctrine of papal primacy will be carried to extremes and the full power of the pope will be so overemphasized that the individual bishops will seem nothing more than functionaries receiving orders, and executive organs of the supreme authority.

In the East, however, even according to Rome's new Oriental Church Law, the duties and powers which in the Latin Church are reserved to the pope alone, are shared between the pope and the patriarchs. Thus the suspicion is eliminated that the pope always and in every case *must* use the full powers of his general, immediate, and ordinary jurisdiction over the entire Church. In many cases he can in fact leave the exercise of this power to others without abdicating his rights or suffering a diminution of his prerogatives. Thus even today there is recognized in the Catholic East an ecclesiastical constitution which conforms more to the factual situation of the first Christian centuries than to the centralized governmental system as it has evolved in the West.

Before the schism, the Eastern patriarchs enjoyed a far-reaching autonomy for the regulation of their internal affairs. The pope as the head of the universal Church intervened only in rare cases, as for example when the preservation of the true faith or the maintenance of ecclesiastical order required it. The pope at that time possessed the same plentitude of power as he does today, but it is an undeniable historical fact that this fullness of power was not used in the same measure before the Eastern schism as it is today. The actual and full use of the papal prerogatives is not essential for the exercise of the primacy.

Even after the restoration of communion with Rome, which had been interrupted by the schism, the Holy See has recognized in principle the Eastern hierarchical structure as it existed before the schism. And this continued even after the definition of the primacy by the first Vatican Council. Pius IX, in his letter of 1848 to the separated patriarchs and bishops (which we cited earlier), names the restoration of ecclesiastical communion with the See of Peter as the only condition for reunion. While this includes of course submission to the supreme authority of the Holy See, it leaves the hierarchical structure of the Eastern patriarchates untouched. They are free to restore communion with Rome within their own structure. It can be assumed that Pius IX held to this view even after the Vatican Council.

Basic for the Catholic concept of the autonomy of the Eastern patriarchates is the definition of primacy formulated by the Council of Florence, 1439:

> We define that the Holy Apostolic See and the Pope of Rome have primacy over the entire globe and that the Roman Pope himself is the successor to St. Peter, the Prince of the Apostles, and is truly the Vicar of Christ, head of the entire Church, and father and teacher of all Christians. To him, in the person of Peter, has been given the authority by our Lord Jesus Christ to govern the universal Church and to guide it, as this is set down in the acts of the Ecumenical Councils and in the sacred canons.

The document then elaborates on the order of precedence for the Eastern patriarchates, and in this connection the significant sentence is added: "Salvis videlicet privilegiis *omnibus* et iuribus eorum" [preserving *all* their privileges and rights].[5]

To understand the significance of this definition, one has to see it within the framework of the history that preceded it. The question of the primacy was not touched

---

5. J. Gill, *The Council of Florence,* Cambridge 1959, pp. 414–415.

upon in Florence until close to the end of the council. On June 22, 1439, only two weeks before the union was concluded on July 6, Pope Eugene IV presented to the Byzantine Emperor John VIII, Palaeologos, a draft document which said that the pope had the right to call ecumenical councils, and that the Oriental patriarchs were subject to him. The emperor's reaction was a categorical rejection. There was no point, he declared, in even discussing such a proposal; if the pope insisted on it, the Greeks would leave immediately. The pope gave in, presented a new proposal containing a less detailed description of the rights of primacy, and accepted the addition demanded by the Greeks about the preservation of *all* the privileges and rights of the Eastern patriarchs. Thus union was secured. The Greeks were convinced that in practice nothing was changed for them with the exception of the right of appeal to the pope. And indeed the pope did not interfere afterwards in Constantinople in any of the internal affairs of the Greek Church. The definition of Florence, therefore, retained for the Eastern Churches a very far-reaching autonomy just as it had existed before the schism.

The union of Florence set the example for the later unions of important groups of Churches. The reunion of the Ruthenians of the Polish-Lithuanian Federation of States (1595) and that of the Rumanians of Transylvania (1698) were accomplished essentially on the basis of the principles established in Florence. Pope Clemens VIII in his Bull *Decet Romanorum Pontificem,* of February 23, 1596, granted far-reaching autonomy to the Ruthenians and empowered the Metropolitan of Kiev to install bishops on his own discretion without having to obtain confirmations from Rome. Only the Metropolitan himself had to be confirmed by Rome. The Rumanians of Transylvania demanded at their union synod of 1698 that their bishop should be allowed to rule his flock without hindrance or interference. That synod was first ratified by the Emperor Leopold and the Primate of Hungary, Cardinal Kollonicz. Rome consented to the resolution of the Synod.

The Holy See has repeatedly offered union to the Orientals under the conditions of Florence, that is to say, with full protection of their autonomy: in 1624 to the Patriarch Theophanes of Jerusalem, in 1625 to Patriarch Kyrillos Lukaris of Constantinople, and in 1637 to the Greek Patriarch Metrophanes of Alexandria.

Time and again during negotiations for union, Rome promised the Oriental patriarchs and bishops that reunion with Rome would in no way diminish their ranks, and their rights and privileges would be retained intact. Reassurances on this score were given, for example, by Clemens XI to the Coptic Patriarch John XVI. In the pope's letter of April 11, 1703, one can read: "By this salutary decision [union] you would restore to this eminent patriarchal seat its ancient dignity which it once possessed according to the testimony of nearly all witnesses of the Catholic faith." That is to say, the Patriarchate of Alexandria was to be restored to the status it had before the schism. At the end of his letter the pope offers the patriarch even further assurances:

> If, with the help of God, you will carry to completion this laudable and salutary resolve [reunion with Rome], you may rest assured

that we shall remain true to the tradition of
the Holy See which not only preserves undiminished the rights and privileges of the Oriental Churches but protects them and will
even take pains to increase them. We shall
embrace you in the Lord with all proofs of
our benevolence and with the honor which
befits your office and your dignity, and we
shall never neglect doing anything that we
assume may please you and will enhance your
position.[6]

Pope Clemens XII, in 1731, promised the Greek Patriarch Kosmas of Alexandria the full and unrestricted
preservation of his rights in case of reunion: The patriarchal seat of Alexandria would thereby regain its ancient
dignity and splendor; the authority of the patriarch would
in no way be diminished.[7]

Pope Pius VII wrote to the Coptic Patriarch Petrus VII
on July 18, 1815: "We shall see to it most diligently that
the prerogatives and privileges of this See [of Alexandria]
will be scrupulously preserved." And Pius VII quoted
Pope Leo the Great: "Of the dignity of the See of Alexandria not an item shall be lost."[8]

Pope Leo XII, who in 1824 made a serious though vain
attempt to restore the Coptic Catholic patriarchate promised the patriarch to be given "all honors, privileges and

6. S.J.P. Trossen, *Les Relations du Patriarche Copte Jean XVI avec
Rome*, Luxemberg, 1948, pp. 171–172.
    7. Appendix, *Bullarium Pontificum Sacrae Congregationis de Propa-
ganda Fide*, Vol. II, p. 43 (n.d.).
    8. R. De Martinis, *Juris Pontifici de Propaganda Fide*, Part I, Vol. IV,
p. 530.

prerogatives, all titles and all authorities" which have their origin either in the sacred canons or have become custom by right of tradition.[9]

When, in extraordinary circumstances, the Holy See saw itself constrained to intervene directly by appointing patriarchs and bishops, it made it a point to emphasize every time that this was an exceptional case, not intended to infringe on the traditional rights of the Orientals with respect to the election of patriarchs and bishops—as was most recently done at the appointment of the present Maronite Patriarch.

The great union-minded Pope Leo XIII, who perhaps more than any other man understood the Orient and was resolved to do it justice in all things, sweepingly and solemnly promised the Oriental patriarchs the full protection of their traditional privileges. In his Moto Proprio *Auspicia Rerum* of March 19, 1896, he said: "No one can fail to observe how fit and appropriate it is that the Catholics do not withhold from their patriarchates any of the guarantees [praesidia] and honors [ornamenta] with which this office is so richly endowed by the non-Catholics [of the East]."[10] In his encyclical *Praeclara gratulationis* of June 20, 1894, Leo XIII declared solemnly:

> There is no reason to fear that either we or our successors would thereby [in case of union] abrogate even one of your rights and patriarchal privileges or any of the liturgical customs of your Churches. For it has always been and will always remain the intent and custom

---

9. *Ibid.* p. 651.
10. *Acta S. Sedis* 28, 1895-96, p. 586.

of the Holy See in everything that is proper
and useful to show wide consideration for
the individuality and the customs of every
people.[11]

The primacy of the pope is thus seen as compatible with
the existence of Churches that are part of the one universal
Church and to which, within the framework of the whole
and under the authority of the Bishop of Rome, a far-
reaching autonomy for the regulation of their internal
affairs is due. The "consideration for the individuality and
the customs of every people," which Leo XIII described
as characteristic for the popes' manner of governing, has
been and still is being generously applied with respect to
the Christian East. It should, however, be applied also to
those peoples of the West who through an unfortunate
chain of circumstances, or because of the guilt or failure
of men in times past, have for centuries been severed from
the center of Christian unity. Throughout all this time they
have been accustomed to govern themselves in ecclesiastical matters. If it ever should come to a corporate union
—and that must be our goal—would it not be expecting
too much to demand from them the acceptance of the
same centralized system of government which is customary
in the Western Catholic Church today? It does not have to
be thus. The existence of the autonomous patriarchates in
the Catholic East proves this point.

Understanding for the importance of the Office of Peter
in the Church is growing more and more with our Protestant brethren. They ask of course, as Otto Karrer writes,
that: First of all, there must be assurance that this office

11. *Acta S. Sedis* 26, 1893-94, p. 709.

of the Church will be devoted to service, not to an authoritarian wielding of power; secondly, that the Church rests not only on the Apostolic Office but also, and equally so, on the "prophets" (by which is here meant the general priesthood); and thirdly that the bishops must preserve solidarity among themselves and with the Office of Peter for the sake of Church unity, but cannot be replaced by a papal autocracy because they are not delegates of the Office of Peter but successors of the college of the Apostles, and therefore also bearers of the "magisterium ordinarium."[12] The factual recognition of the hierarchical structure of the Eastern Church points the way to the realization of such yearnings.

Unity of faith, finally, is the essential and indispensable prerequisite for the reunion of Christians in the true Church.

How does the Church understand this unity in faith and doctrine? Is it understood to mean that all Catholics in all the world must formulate the truths of their faith in exactly the same way? That no nuances of language may be permitted in the vernacular presentation of the deposit of faith? Does it mean that any and every "home-grown" theology, taking into consideration the intellectual individualities of the various races in East and West, is to be a priori excluded?

Certainly no differences in faith can be admitted in matters of substance. But the reality of the faith is so rich and so lofty as compared to our human capacity for comprehension that it can never be completely exhausted or reduced to formulas. It can, however, be presented in

---

12. Roesle-Cullman, *Begegnung der Christen* ("Meeting of the Christians"), Frankfurt/Main, 1959, pp. 23-24.

various ways. Our Western theology which has been formed out of *our* Western intellectual characteristics cannot be permitted to be regarded as the final word. There may also be forms of comprehending the faith which are the product of other and different intellectual backgrounds.

The characteristic theology of the Christian East is a direct descendant from the spirit of the early Greek Fathers. And the Catholic Church's attitude toward the Christian East and its theology is proof that the Church is willing to admit variations in expression and emphasis even while holding fast to the absolute necessity of unity in faith. Once more, the best illustration for that fact is the Council of Florence. Discussions were permitted there on matters of faith which had already been defined, such as the "filioque" (the doctrine of the Holy Spirit proceeding from the Father and the Son). What had to be determined was whether there existed substantial differences in concepts or whether it was merely a question of different modes of expression, variations in emphasis, a looking at the same truth from varying points of view. The decree of union arrived at by the Council of Florence shows the result of this discussion, namely a full acceptance of the "Greek way" to perceive this mystery and to put it into words:

> The proofs from Holy Scripture and the testimony of many holy Doctors of the Church of both the East and the West were brought forth. Some of them speak of the Holy Spirit as proceeding from the Father *and* the Son, others as proceeding from the Father *through*

the Son. All understand it in the same way
though they express it in different words.

The specific concern which the Greeks had at heart was to
preserve the oneness of the "causation" of the Holy Spirit.
Father and Son are not a two-fold causal principle of the
Holy Spirit, but only one. For that reason they preferred
the formula "from the Father through the Son" without,
however, excluding the Son as a principal cause of the
Holy Spirit. The Latins put the emphasis more on the
importance of the Son in the procession of the Holy Spirit
without, however, intending to put themselves in objective
contradiction to the Greeks. All this became clear during
the long and patient discussions which were carried on in
a spirit of sincere willingness for mutual understanding.

On the doctrine of purgatory an agreement of mutual
understanding also was reached after long discussion. The
Greeks admitted the possibility of purification after death
through "purgative punishments," but the word "purga-
torium" was not pressed on them. Had the principles of
Florence been better observed at later union discussions,
many an outcome might have been different.

It has thus been shown that the doctrines of the faith
can be expressed in various ways. If this is true for the
East, there is no reason why it should be different in the
West. The Christians of the various denominations have
for centuries passed each other by. Sad as it is, they have
avoided entering into conversation, into dialogue with
each other. And so each side has evolved its own theological language in order to present in some way God's
impenetrable mysteries, an undertaking which must always remain inadequate. The result was that we talked,

not with but past, each other; we no longer spoke the same language even when we used the same idiom. Now we must, first of all, slowly and cautiously begin to grope our way toward one another again through patient dialogue, always in a desire to understand the other. In France and Germany such dialogue has been carried on without much ado for a long time between Catholic and Protestant theologians. Not infrequently the theologians discovered after days of discussion that basically they meant the same thing even though they expressed what they meant in entirely different terms. Sometimes, of course, they had to admit with resignation that certain differences of opinion could indeed not be bridged.

Once Christians on both sides make a real effort to understand each other's language and even attempt to speak it themselves, it will perhaps become obvious that some of our ostensible differences in faith are only apparent differences. At the Evangelical Church Congress in Munich, 1959, the Swiss Reformed theologian, Dr. Jean Louis Leuba, gave a lecture, which received much attention, on the question "Must there be different Churches?" He suggested that the seemingly unbridgeable differences between the denominations be subjected to an exacting examination. It is conceivable, he maintained, that the doctrines of the Catholic Church, once they were expressed in the terminology of the Evangelical theologians, would be perfectly acceptable to Evangelical Christians.

Certainly, we would have to ask the other side to accept the *substance* of the Catholic faith undiminished, and to acknowledge that the Catholic Church represents correctly the deposit of Revelation in its doctrinal pronouncements. But we ask ourselves: Do we have the right to impose our theological language on them and to require them to abandon their own particular style in theological matters which has become familiar to them over a long period of time? We are all too easily tempted to do just that. It has even been suggested that full, unequivocal clarity in theological discussions could be guaranteed only by the exclusive use of Latin and its specialized terminology at all official occasions!

A truly Catholic willingness to concede the possibility of a self-developed theology for others can prepare the way for unity. The definitions of Florence, which prove the possibility of such a solution, point the way even today toward the kind of reunion that may be realizable. The restoration of union consisted then, as it does today, of the coming home to the one true Church of Jesus Christ by those who are separated, that is to say, those whose ancestors arbitrarily severed themselves from the Church. There is in the union decree of Florence not a word that would allude to "return," penance, renunciation, or absolution. *The lost unity is being restored.* The Church rejoices that her sons, who up to then were feuding with one another, have returned to unity in peace. "The wall that heretofore separated the Western and Eastern Churches from each other is torn down and peace and harmony have returned."

Would it not also be possible today, when it is the task of the hour to prepare the corporate reunion of entire groups, to avoid hurtful expressions without surrendering fundamental Catholic concepts of reunion? Pope John XXIII obviously was intent on just such an approach in every word he spoke. In his Apostolic Letter *Superni Dei Nutu* of Pentecost, 1960, he created, in addition to the commissions which were to undertake the preparation of his council, a separate secretariat for those who, though separated from the Apostolic See, "also bear the honored name Christians" so that they may "more easily find the way to that union which Jesus Christ implored with incessant prayer from his heavenly Father."

So much is certain: Reunion must not be a capitulation for anyone nor for us a triumph over a vanquished opponent. The others shall be allowed to bring with them into the common house of the Father whatever is rightly dear and precious to them. They need not relinquish anything of true value. On the contrary, they shall find everything fulfilled and complete in the true Church.

The Church is *catholic*—which means all-embracing: We do not have the right to restrict it to our own Western mentality and to force our characteristics on others as if ours were the only Catholic characteristics.

We do not have the right to narrow, anymore than God himself narrows, the gate to the Church which alone assures salvation.

We do not have the right to bar by human statute the road of salvation to other men.

※   ※   ※

Lord, you have united the various peoples in the confession of your name. We pray to you for the Christian peoples of the East. Remembering the eminent place which they once held in your Church, we implore you: Awake in them the longing to have this place restored to them and to form with us one single fold under the guidance of one and the same shepherd. Grant them the grace that, together with us, they may penetrate ever more deeply into the teachings of their holy Church Fathers who are also our fathers in the faith. Preserve them from any fault which might alienate them from us. May the spirit of harmony and love which marks your presence among the faithful hasten the dawn of the day on which our prayers will mingle with theirs, so that every nation and every tongue will acknowledge and glorify our Lord Jesus Christ, your son. Amen.

(Pope Benedict XV)

3

Johannes
Chrysostomus, OSB

THE CATHOLIC
CHURCH AND
THE ORTHODOX

WHEN WE CATHOLICS of the West speak of Christian schism, we think most of the time of that fateful break that parted the Western Christian nations into two main confessions: Catholic and Evangelical, or Protestant. It is understandable that this rupture is most painful to every sincere Christian, whether Catholic or Protestant. However, we should not forget that this separation is not the only one which has inflicted a grievous wound on Christianity. From the point of view of what the universal Church was intended to be, the separation of numerous Eastern Christians from Rome is not only more painful, but is also the greater calamity. And it is all the more painful because the Catholics and the Eastern Churches that are separated from Rome have so much doctrinal inheritance in common that it would seem easy to achieve union. The many failures of such attempts in the course of the centuries, however, reveal that this is not quite so.

For a Christian in the West who at every step is confronted with the consequences of our religious disunion, it may not be easy to feel the Eastern schism with equal intensity, if only because the East is more remote to him. Yet as Catholics, that is to say, as members of a world-wide Church, we cannot afford to remain isolated in our narrow provincial ways, the less so in an age where all isolations break down and the world moves closer and closer to some kind of unity. It certainly is of decisive importance that, as we pray Christ's own prayer, "That all may be one" (John 17: 21), we put ourselves in union with the all-embracing—the world-embracing—charity of Christ. This charity, however, will truly come to life only when it arises from our concern for the brethren on the other side of the great divide, from our knowledge of their history and their life in our day.

Therefore, we shall ask ourselves how the Eastern Church came into being, how it developed, what our differences are, where the areas lie which we have in common, and what possibilities of rapprochement exist between Rome and this separated branch of Christendom.

What Do We Mean by the Eastern Church?

The term "Eastern Church" is often heard these days, but it is not always clear to all what is meant by it.

In its widest meaning, the word is used to denote the entirety of all Christian Churches that have sprung up on the territory of the Eastern Roman empire, or which have been founded by these Churches.

In this respect, the distinction between the Eastern and the Western Church goes back to the division of the old Roman Empire into two empires, East and West. Perhaps it would be better not to speak of the Eastern Church but of the Eastern Churches, for Eastern Christianity does not constitute an entity today in the same way as does the Roman Catholic Church; it consists instead of a number of Churches, all independent of one another.

In this widest meaning of the word, the term "Eastern Church" or "Eastern Churches" embraces all Christians of the East, those separated from Rome as well as those who live in union with Rome. The latter are often called Uniates.

Most Eastern, or Oriental, Christians are separated from Rome. Those that are in communion with Rome are a numerically rather weak group. Since the Roman Catholic Church accords equal recognition to all rites, the Orientals that are united with Rome are, of course, Catholics just as any other Catholics of the Roman rite. It is therefore wrong to ask someone: "Are you Catholic or Uniate?" Any Christian living in communion with Rome is a Catholic. The right question would be: "To what rite do you belong?" By rite we understand the whole body of religious customs and ceremonies, traditional usages, ecclesiastical laws—in one word: the entirety of religious life.

While all Catholics, irrespective of the rite to which they belong, are completely one in faith, they differ according to the rites of the various groups. The rite, however, constitutes a bond between the Oriental Catholics and the Orientals separated from Rome, and thus represents a bridge for future rapprochement and reunion.

There are five distinct rites within the Eastern Church: Byzantine, Alexandrian, East-Syrian, West-Syrian, and Armenian. In each of these rites there are Catholics as well as Christians not in union with Rome. By far the most Eastern Christians belong to the Byzantine rite. Therefore, we shall in the following pages first of all speak of the Byzantine Church.

Origin of the Divisions

As is commonly known, the main theological discussions regarding the most important dogmas of Christianity took place in the East between the fourth and fifth centuries. Here lived the great theologians and saints: Athanasius, Basilius, Cyril of Alexandria, Gregory Nazianzus, and many others who today are revered in the West as much as in the East as Fathers and Doctors of the Church.

The first important councils were held in the East, the councils that defined the dogma of the three Divine Persons (Nicea 325, and Constantinople 381), and the dogma of the divinity and humanity of Christ (Ephesus 431, and Chalcedon 451). In the Second Ecumenical Council of Constantinople (381) the text of the creed was drawn up, the same text which even today is being used in the divine liturgies of both the East and the West.

For centuries, the Orthodox East battled side by side with the Church of Rome against all heresies. However, as early as the fifth century, some of the Eastern Churches succumbed to the influence of erroneous doctrines and cut themselves off from the universal Church. Among these were, for example, the Churches of Egypt, Armenia, and Ethiopia—which adopted the heresy of monophysitism—the recognition of a divine nature only in Christ. The original monophysitism has considerably declined today. The humanity of Christ is no longer entirely denied, but by now the traditional separation remains intact and is hard to overcome.

The majority of the Eastern Churches, however, remained loyal to the Orthodox teachings. In contrast to the various believers, they preferred to call themselves "ortho-

dox" (of the true faith) and also "catholic" (world-wide),
the name by which the Western Church was known. Even
today, the Western Church claims for itself the term
"orthodox" in its original meaning.[1]

The solidarity in the one Church and the common stand
against heresy could not prevent, however, the relations
between Rome and Byzantium from becoming less and
less friendly. Strong political, cultural, and psychological
motives were at work to bring about a mutual alienation.
The theologians of Rome and Byzantium expressed themselves in different terminologies, a fact which not infrequently led to misunderstandings or even mutual suspicions.

A serious split developed in the ninth century when
Rome refused recognition to the Byzantine Patriarch
Photius. He in turn accused the Roman Church with the
countercharge that its doctrine was no longer authentically
pure. Even though this breach was later healed again, the
remedy was only temporary and external. The deep-seated
estrangement between Rome and Byzantium continued.

In the year 1050 came the final break. The emissary of
the pope placed on the altar of the Church of Divine Wisdom (Hagia Sophia) in Constantinople the bull of excommunication against the Byzantine patriarch.

The rupture widened and spread until it resulted in the
dissolution of the union with Rome not only in Byzantium
itself but also in the other Oriental patriarchates as well

---

1. As in this prayer from the Canon of the Latin rite Mass: ". . . accept
and bless these gifts . . . which . . . we offer Thee for Thy holy Catholic
Church: which vouchsafe to guard, unite, and govern throughout the
whole world, together with Thy servant, our Pope . . . our Bishop . . .
as also all orthodox believers and professors of the Catholic and Apostolic
faith."

as in the Churches that had been founded by them. A union of centuries had been broken. Subsequently, the name "Orthodox" (now narrowed in its application as compared to the original meaning), came to be the denominational designation of the Churches in union with Constantinople and separated from Rome.

Sometimes, the word "Eastern Church" is collectively used to denote only the Orthodox Churches; but because this could lead to confusion, we shall here stay with the term "Orthodox Church."

Orthodox and Catholic

Since the two Churches were united for over a thousand years, they naturally have a great deal of their heritage of faith in common. The saints and doctors of the Church of the early period are as greatly revered in the East as in the West. The dogmatic decisions of the seven ecumenical councils (from the First Ecumenical Council of Nicea in 325 to the Second Ecumenical Council of Nicea in 787) are unanimously accepted by both Churches as an expression of the infallible Church of Christ, as indisputable, unalterable, absolutely binding norms of faith. From this fact derives a much greater dogmatic kinship between the Catholic Church and the Orthodox Church than exists, for example, between Catholics and Protestants, or between Protestants and Orthodox.

This agreement on fundamental principles produces, in consequence, a Catholic-Orthodox consensus on a number of points which constitute *differences* in faith between the Catholic Church and the Protestant Churches.

The Orthodox Church, like the Catholic Church, considers itself the only true Church. It believes itself to be in possession of the full truth. The fact that some Orthodox Churches have for many years participated in the Protestant ecumenical movement, does not mean that they are prepared to look upon the various Protestant communities as equivalent to their own Churches. The representatives of the Orthodox Churches at ecumenical conferences have repeatedly explained and emphasized this point. If such a recognition had been required of the participating Churches, the Orthodox would have had no choice but to withdraw from the ecumenical movement. In principle, the Orthodox adhere to the same concept of the Church as do Catholics; they merely apply it to their own Church. Thus they represent, so to speak, within the overwhelmingly Protestant ecumenical movement the Catholic concept of the Church. There are, of course, also Orthodox theologians who maintain a somewhat vague position on this point, but the traditional Orthodox concept, as it is also expressed in the rite of acceptance into the Orthodox Church, is essentially the same as the Catholic concept.

Both confessions share a very similar understanding of the visible hierarchy whose duty it is to lead and to teach the faithful. According to Orthodox interpretation, the sacrament of Holy Orders confers a specific character, just as in the Catholic tradition. The Orthodox Church also has the same three degrees of sacramental ordination: bishops, priests, and deacons.

Furthermore, the Orthodox Church has the same understanding of the Mass: it believes that in this sacred action the one sacrifice of Christ on Calvary is made present in an unbloody, mysterious way.

It holds, just as the Catholic Church does, that the

Mass can be valid only when it is offered by a validly ordained priest, that is to say, a priest consecrated by a bishop who is linked to the Apostles through an unbroken chain of succession. This also implies that the Orthodox Church shares fully and completely the Catholic teaching on the apostolic succession. It follows that all bishops and priests of the Orthodox Church are able to offer the Mass validly and to administer validly the sacraments to the faithful. When an Orthodox priest or bishop becomes a Catholic he stands, by virtue of his ordination, in one and the same order with the Catholic priests or bishops.

The Orthodox Church also recognizes the same seven sacraments as the Catholic Church.

Veneration of the saints is very strongly emphasized in the Orthodox Church. Their churches are filled with images (icons) of saints and angels. Candles are burned before them and incense is used in their honor. The icons are kissed, and people kneel before them. The veneration accorded the saints and their images is a characteristic feature of the Orthodox Church. It probably can be explained by the fact that in the eighth and ninth centuries the Church had to wage a severe struggle against the opponents of the icon cult.

The Orthodox devotion to the saints is properly founded, and is being carried on in such a way that (just as in the Western Church) the saints are honored for their fidelity to Christ and their love for him. Orthodox doctrine, the same as the Catholic doctrine, is Christ-centered throughout.

Every Orthodox Christian has a special devotion to the Mother of God. This distinct Marian piety forms a bridge between the two confessions. It would be hard to say where the enthusiasm for the Mother of God is greater, in the Latin West or in the Byzantine East. Even though the Orthodox have fewer defined dogmas in regard to the Mother of God, the veneration of Mary is not in any way less for that reason. Countless Marian feasts dot the Orthodox Church year, and there are about two hundred types of icons of the Mother of God which are accorded liturgical recognition.

Liturgical texts are full of praises and invocations of the Mother of God who, time and again, is hailed as "the purest virgin," "the only immaculate," "the perpetual refuge of sinners." The most often used invocation, "Holy Mother of God, save us," is repeated frequently in every service in honor of the Holy Virgin.

The doctrine of the bodily assumption of the Mother of God into heaven is accepted by most of the Orthodox, especially in Russia.

Monasticism likewise is esteemed in the Orthodox Church in the same way as it is in the Catholic Church. Orthodox monasticism is not divided into various orders, and this fact distinguishes its form from that in the Catholic West. But the appreciation which monasticism enjoys within Orthodox Christianity, it is even greater than the esteem monasticism is accorded in Western Christianity. Orthodox bishops, practically without exception, belong to the monastic order.

As in the Catholic Church, prayers for the deceased are considered by the Orthodox as an indispensable duty of the faithful. It is customary after the death of a relative to have Mass offered forty times for the eternal peace of the departed soul. Devotions for the dead (*panychiden*) are very popular with the Orthodox faithful. In addition, various days are set aside for the commemoration of the dead on which special prayers are said for them.

All this proves clearly the close kinship between Catholic and Orthodox doctrine. Yet, in spite of all this, there are many differences which cannot be overlooked.

Dogmatic Differences

Before we go into this matter, we have to define clearly what we mean by "dogma." By "dogma" is meant an article of faith which has been declared absolutely binding, presented by the Church to the faithful as a truth contained in divine revelation. A dogma, therefore, can never be revoked, revised, or altered in any way. It is conceivable, however, that in the course of time a deeper understanding of a certain dogma may be reached, and it is then possible to define additional dogmas to explain or supplement the earlier ones. Never, however, within the framework of one and the same confession, can one dogma contradict another.

In this understanding of dogma Catholics and Orthodox also agree fully. Only on the question of *how* dogmas are defined and proclaimed, do their views differ. Both agree that it is the business of the Church to determine what is dogma, but as to the organ within the Church that should proclaim dogmas, they hold differing opinions.

According to Catholic thinking, a dogma may be proclaimed either by an ecumenical council (a council representing the entire Church), arriving at its decisions in consensus with the pope, or by the pope alone—but only if, in his capacity as the supreme teacher of the Church, he is pronouncing a truth as an article of faith binding the entire universal Church.

In all this, pope and council can of course never be separated from or set against each other. The pope, the ecumenical council, and the Church in its entirety are one. Since Christ intended to endow His Church with the charisma of infallibility, the pope and the bishops assembled in an ecumenical council of the entire Church must also be infallible in their collective role as supreme teacher of the Church.

Orthodox theologians, however, are not agreed even among themselves on their position as to the actual organ of the Church in which infallibility is vested. Traditional Orthodox theology has the same concept of an ecumenical council as has the Catholic Church—although its concept is limited to the first seven ecumenical councils.

Modern Orthodox theologians, not entirely free from Protestant influences, would like to make the infallibility of ecumenical councils dependent on the consent of the entire Church to their decisions. In what manner this consent of the whole Church is to be obtained remains hazy. The infallibility of the pope, however, is rejected by all the Orthodox.

The result of this attitude is that on the part of the Orthodox only that may be admitted as absolutely unchangeable truth which has been resolved by the first seven ecumenical councils. Since all these councils (from 325 to 787) are recognized by the Catholic Church as ecumenical and infallible, their decisions are considered by the Catholic Church as unalterable and absolutely binding dogmas. Up to this point there is full agreement.

Now, since the Orthodox Church does not recognize

any other councils as ecumenical, and since some of their theologians even deny the possibility of calling an ecumenical council until the time when the schism in Christianity is healed, it follows that the Orthodox Church has not been in the position to formulate any dogmas which the Catholic Church could contradict.

One cannot, therefore, speak of any dogmatic disagreement between the Catholic and the Orthodox Church, as though there were such things as Orthodox dogmas opposed to Catholic dogmas. If that were indeed the case, there could hardly be any hope for agreement.

The dogmatic differences we do have consist of different interpretations of the doctrines of the first seven councils or, to phrase it in another way, in the rejection by the Orthodox of some dogmas as they were later defined by the Catholic Church.

Even though the Orthodox are more or less agreed among themselves on this rejection today, this non-acceptance is no absolute duty for them. If they would choose no longer to adhere to this rejection, they would not commit a violation of an Orthodox dogma, but would turn their backs only on theological opinions that have become traditional for no other reason than that they were widely held.

While the Catholic Church did define some dogmas since the separation took place, it considers these definitions to be in agreement with the ancient dogmas. The Orthodox, however, hold some of these to be innovations and in contrast to ecclesiastical tradition. The difficulty is that the Catholic Church considers these later proclaimed dogmas just as absolutely binding as the earlier ones, and for this reason it cannot reduce them in any way—on the

contrary, it will constantly have to require their acceptance by the Orthodox as an indispensable prerequisite for
union. To hope that the Catholic Church could change its
position on this point, would be illusory; it would be tantamount to assuming that it could surrender its conviction
of being the true Church.

On the other side stands the fact that there has grown
among Orthodox theologians the habit of considering
these dogmas as unacceptable to the Orthodox, although
there existed—200 to 300 years ago—quite different theological concepts among the Orthodox hierarchy and theologians in regard to the same questions.

Today there are four Catholic dogmas which usually
are pointed out as areas of difference between Catholicism
and Orthodoxy:

1. *The dogma of the immaculate conception of the Most
Blessed Virgin Mary:* the doctrine that Mary, from the
first moment of her existence in the womb of her mother,
was preserved from original sin by the Holy Spirit.

This doctrine diminishes in no way, of course, the redemptive act of Jesus Christ, as is sometimes erroneously
assumed by people who have little acquaintance with the
doctrines of the Catholic Church. Even the Mother of
God could not achieve this grace without redemption
through Jesus Christ. The effect of the grace of redemption in her case, however, was to *preserve* her from sin,
while in other men it is to *cleanse* them from sin. It was,
so to speak, a pre-redemption in view of the coming act
of salvation by Christ.

It is difficult to understand that the Orthodox Church
rejects this particular dogma while it continues to express
in such lavish manner its devotion to the Mother of

God, unceasingly praising her as "the most pure," "entirely without sin," "immaculate," "the only pure." This phenomenon becomes even more inexplicable when we remember that the liturgical texts of the feasts of Mary in the Orthodox Church offer the clearest evidence of this doctrine. The Orthodox pray in the office of September 8, the feast of the Birth of Mary: "We hail thy holy birth and revere thy immaculate conception, O bride, called by God."

On November 21, the feast of the Presentation of Mary in the Temple, we read: "Before thy conception thou wast sanctified by God, O pure one, and after thou wast born on earth, thou wast brought to Him as an oblation."

There is evidence for the fact that in the early centuries the Church of the East professed the doctrine of the immaculate conception of the Mother of God. Only in the seventeenth century did those who deny this doctrine achieve dominance in the Orthodox Church.

This can be seen with particular clarity in an example from the history of the Russian Church: In the seventeenth century, there occurred a split within the Russian Church on account of liturgical reform. The opponents of the reform withdrew from the official Orthodoxy and formed a denomination of their own. They intended to remain in the Orthodox tradition but broke with the official hierarchy because they considered it too fond of innovation. This dissident group was called the Old Ritualists. Their program was to preserve everything as it had been before the liturgical reform.

In the middle of the last century, the Old Ritualists brought all their teachings together in a book which they considered the official book of their doctrines. In it one can read about the Mother of God as follows: "Her conception was truly immaculate because purified and sanctified by God. . . . Whoever thinks differently of her cannot be accepted in our communion. . . . Shame on those who blaspheme the throne of the Cherubim! Barred from us shall be the hellish heretical mouth that utters such intolerable blasphemy against the Ever-blessed Virgin."

We can see from this that the rejection of the Catholic dogma is not supported by a very long tradition within the Orthodox Church. The acceptance of this dogma by the Orthodox would, therefore, not be a breach of truly Orthodox tradition.

2. *The dogma that the Holy Spirit proceeds from the Father and the Son.* For a long time, this dogma of the Catholic Church was considered by the Orthodox as the main block in the way of a rapprochement between the two Churches. Patriarch Photius already opposed this doctrine by calling it an innovation, and he maintained that the Holy Spirit proceeds from the Father only.

Tempers were especially agitated when the word "filioque" ("and from the Son") was inserted into the Credo of the Western liturgy. That was still before the final separation between the Western and Eastern Churches in 1054. Although the Church Fathers of the East also professed the doctrine that the Holy Spirit proceeds from the Father *through* the Son—which, in essence, means the same as "from the Father *and* the Son"—the opinion gained acceptance by the Orthodox theologians that the "filioque" doctrine was a heresy which under no circumstances could be allowed to be sanctioned by the Orthodox Church. The four Oriental Patriarchs, in a message to all Orthodox Christians in 1848, wrote on the "filioque" problem the following verdict: "This innovation is truly a heresy. Its adherents, whoever they may be, are heretics."

But half a century later, a well-known Russian professor of theology on the basis of more advanced knowledge of Orthodox theological scholarship, was able to arrive at a quite different judgment: "It is a blot on Russian theology," he wrote, "that it continues to label the 'filioque' as a heresy, since it has been established beyond a doubt that this doctrine was held as pious belief by the Fathers and Doctors of the Church of both the East and the West."

Even though the "filioque" doctrine is still being rejected by Orthodox theologians today, it is not being done any more with the same severity as in earlier times. It is hardly possible to conclude that it still should represent any unsurmountable difficulties.

3. *The Catholic dogma of purgatory.* As we have already seen, the practice of praying for the deceased is very widely in use in the Orthodox Church. This alone proves that the Orthodox Church cannot reject the Catholic concept of purgatory in the same way as Protestant Christians do. More accurately expressed, what we have here is not so much a rejection of the doctrine of purgatory as a different concept of it. Purgatory as, so to speak, a third "place" besides heaven and hell, is rejected. But neither does the Catholic Church insist on the concept of purgatory as necessarily a *place* in the literal meaning of the word; it rather thinks of it as a *state of being* for the purpose of purgation. In addition, in relation to liberation from this state of being, the Orthodox put emphasis on the prayers of the living rather than on the suffering of the souls of the departed.

In a commentary on this subject in the *Lives of the*

Saints, published in 1906 by the Holy Synod of the Russian Orthodox Church, we find the following statement about the condition of the souls of the departed: "If the soul of the deceased person has more sins than good works, it is being temporarily detained by the demons and remains in their captivity where God permits it to be tormented by them until He grants the soul liberation from these pains."

We see here a concept of the hereafter which touches on that of Catholic teachings on purgatory.

The three points which we have here mentioned are no longer considered as insurmountable by contemporary Orthodox theologians. The fourth point, however, they do consider unsurmountable.

4. *The dogma of papal jurisdictional primacy and, related to it, the infallibility of the pope.* This dogma is sometimes presented in two aspects: primacy and infallibility. But because the doctrine of infallibility, declared a dogma as recently as 1870, is logically a part of the doctrine of papal primacy, which became a dogma much earlier, we shall treat these two aspects together.

If one admits that, for the sake of the unity of his Church, Christ intended to establish the office of a supreme head, then it is only logical to assume that He endowed this office with the grace of freedom from error in order to guarantee its unity not only in government, but also in doctrine. It is interesting to note that some Orthodox theologians without any hesitation admit the logical connection between the doctrine of papal primacy and papal infallibility; they also acknowledge that both the doctrine of papal primacy and of papal infallibility were already held by some of the Fathers of the early

Church. The Russian professor of theology and Church historian, Bolotov, for example, relates the teaching of Pope Leo III, Doctor of the Church in the fifth century, who enjoys equal esteem in both the Catholic and Orthodox Church, in the following sentences:

> The Apostle Peter is the foundation of the Holy Church, a mediator between Christ and the Church as a whole; in him are concentrated all the gifts of grace which came to the other Apostles only through him.
>
> The fullness of grace and power is conferred first on Peter and then it flows through him, as through the head, into the entire body of the Church. The primacy of the Apostle Peter is an eternal institution because the truth of his confession of faith is eternal.
>
> And just as Christ is the son of the living God in all eternity, so also can Peter, once he has assumed the reins of Government, not divest himself of this office. There is no doubt that, invisibly, Peter still rules the flock of Christ today; visibly, however, he governs the Church through his successors in the See of Rome in which his power lives on and from which his authority radiates. Because the entire Church is built on the rock of Peter, anyone who strays from this rock places himself outside the Mystical Body of Christ—that is to say, outside the Church. (Bolotov, *Lectures on the History of the Ancient Church* [in Russian], St. Petersburg, 1913, Vol. III, p. 281).

A few pages later the same theologian states that in the teachings of St. Leo all the assumptions for the Vatican dogma are already contained. Naturally, like the other Orthodox, Bolotov personally rejected both papal primacy and papal infallibility; but his testimony is important because it shows us clearly that the doctrines of primacy and infallibility are not just inventions of a later period, but were already taught in the times of the early Fathers.

With this established, the thesis of the total unacceptability of these doctrines is put in question. Even if only *one* of the Doctors of the Church (and there were others) clearly professes these doctrines, it is impossible simply to reject them as heresies. We are left, therefore, not with the irreconcilability of these doctrines with those of the Orthodox, but with the strong repugnance of today's Orthodox for acceptance of these doctrines.

Psychological Difficulties

As we have stated earlier, psychological motives played an important role in preparing the separation between Rome and Byzantium. The mutual distrust between the Greeks and the Latins, their different intellectual interests, political tensions, especially strong since the restoration of Western imperialism at the time of Charlemagne—all that contributed to the rise of an adverse climate which threatened even the ecclesiastical unity between the East and the West. Cultural developments, differing in the East from those in the West, also produced different forms of theological thinking which not infrequently led to the point where both sides no longer understood each other properly, and this produced the suspicion of heresy.

This mutual estrangement, combined with a growing distrust, increased after the rupture of 1045. It must be frankly admitted here that the blame for this mutual estrangement must be shared by both sides. Pope John XXIII clearly expressed this in his address to the Roman pastors on June 29, 1959, when he spoke of the efforts for Christian unity: "We do not intend to conduct a trial of the past. We do not want to prove who was right and who was wrong. The responsibilities are divided. All we want to say is: Let us come together! Let us make an end of our divisions."

Especially great harm was done to the relations between Western and Eastern Christianity by the Fourth Crusade (1204). The crusaders, instead of fighting the infidels (which was the purpose of the crusade), attacked and sacked Constantinople, in order to set up a Latin empire there. Even though they acted against the expressed will of the pope, they nonetheless appeared to the Greeks as the representatives of Western Christianity who, instead of helping the hard-pressed Christians of the East against the common enemy, extended their own power at the expense of the Eastern Christians. The numerous sacrileges committed by the crusaders (including desecration of Orthodox Churches) imbued the Byzantines with a deep hatred for the Christians of the West. In their eyes the latter had ceased to be Christian. The invasions of Russia by Western so-called "Christian" knights in the same century, following immediately after that country's devastation by the Tartars, also produced a deep and abiding anti-Roman bias. And it was in consequence of this anti-Roman sentiment that the reunion with Rome, which was signed by the Greek and Russian hierarchies at the Council of Florence in 1493, was rejected.

The detailed clarification of the dogmatic differences at that council (the "filioque" question alone had consumed eight months), in consequence of which the Orthodox hierarchs and theologians had been moved to consent to reunion, was in vain because the masses of the people lived in such a state of anti-Roman feeling that in Byzantium the saying made the rounds at that time, "Better the turban of the Sultan than the tiara of the Pope."

Overcoming the Schism

The main difficulty in the attempt to overcome the schism between the Eastern and the Western Churches lies, as we have seen, in the distrust and the prejudices that exist in the masses of the faithful on both sides. To help reduce this distrust and these prejudices, should be the first task of all who have the unity of Christendom at heart.

The distrust extends no less into the theological sphere. Here it takes the form of looking at the teachings of the other side only through one's own glasses instead of trying to see a problem as the other side understands it.

Cardinal Umberto, who placed the bull of excommunication on the altar of the Church of Divine Wisdom in Constantinople, distorted even then the doctrine of the Greek Church by imputing to it various errors which it did not teach.

But even today there still is not enough effort put forth

to search into the doctrine of the other side, in order to understand it as it is really meant to be understood. Instead, one is too often satisfied with a quite superficial concept. The process of getting to know and to appreciate one another is an indispensable prerequisite for rapprochement. Only an atmosphere of trust and mutual respect can bring about this precondition for union.

Only by contemplating the doctrine of the other side with a calm mind and without preconceived notions, is it possible to realize how close, dogmatically, the two confessions, Catholic and Orthodox, really are. But looked upon with eyes of distrust and suspicion, they seem to be separated by an unbridgeable gulf. Certainly, much that is promising has happened in this realm over the last decades; but it still is not enough.

A case in point is the Vatican dogma of infallibility which, on the Orthodox side, has been adjudged as totally unacceptable. It has been repeatedly said that only its elimination could prepare the way to unity. Yet, it is absolutely illusory even to think of such a possibility. For to assume that something that has been proclaimed as a dogma, could suddenly be declared to be a dogma no longer (or, as some have suggested, a dogma only for some, but not for others), would be nothing less than dogmatic suicide for the Catholic Church. Instead of bandying about such illusory possibilities, the efforts of the theologians must be aimed at elucidating the dogma, so as to explain its formulations in a manner acceptable to the Orthodox tradition.

One passage, especially, in the formulation of the Vatican dogma is rejected by the Orthodox; it is the sentence which says that, in the proclamation of a dogmatic decision, the pope is infallible "ex sese, non autem ex consensu Ecclesiae"—"by virtue of his office, not by virtue of the consensus of the Church."

The Orthodox frequently understand this sentence to mean that according to Catholic doctrine the pope is juxtaposed to the Church, as though he could set himself against the voice of the universal Church. In reality, he is infallible because, as the head of the Church, he is in the position to express validly the voice of the Church, and therefore cannot even be thought of as in contrast or opposition to it.

This example shows that many difficulties might be resolved if they could be discussed in an atmosphere of mutual trust.

To achieve such an atmosphere, however, it is important that not only the theologians engaged in the clarification of dogmatic questions come to a meeting of minds; just as important are the encounters of the faithful laity. Especially in our days where so many Orthodox live in close proximity with Catholics, such meetings could be of great value.

If the Orthodox could feel a truly catholic spirit in their encounters with Catholics, that is to say, a spirit of openness, as becomes a universal Church which also could be their home, a great service would be rendered to the goal of unity. If, on the other hand, they meet with an attitude that equates the Catholic Church with the Western-Latin rite—an attitude which not infrequently can be found among Catholics, even though the popes have emphatically condemned it—then the Orthodox will feel slighted and persist in their rejection of Catholicism.

The cause of Christian unity is, above all, in the hands of God, who will bestow the gift of unity on His Christian people at the time and in the manner He wills. Therefore, prayer for reunion is the most noble and the most important means toward this end—all the more so because all the faithful on each side can make use of it.

4

IRENAEUS TOTZKE, OSB | THE CATHOLIC
CHURCHES OF
THE EAST

WHEN POPE JOHN XXIII convened an ecumenical council, he also moved by this act the Churches of the East into the focus of the West. Unfortunately, however, here in the West our knowledge of the Christian East is next to nil. What the secular press and even the respective Church publications tell us regarding these matters, is often quite contradictory, distorted, or at best half-truth. There is no consensus with respect even to terminology. How many meanings are attached merely to the word "Orthodox"! There is even less understanding of terms such as West-Syrian, East-Syrian, Coptic, and so forth. Also the term "Uniate" is far from being sufficiently clear to all those who use it.

The following pages are intended to be a modest contribution to the clarification of these and other related terms. Special emphasis shall be given to the "Uniates," that is to say those Eastern Christians who recognize the primacy of the pope. We must ask: What are Uniates? Where are they? What is their position in regard to the papacy, to Orthodoxy?

Historical Development

Under the influence of various historical conditions and situations, the *one* Church of Christ developed in various forms and rites. In the West, we have various rites of the Latin cult-language: Roman, Ambrosian, Mozarabic, Gallican, and others; in the East there are the rites of the various cultural spheres of the ancient world: Syrian, Egyptian, Persian, and others—each with its own cult language. These diversities do not by themselves constitute a division or dissension within the universal Church, for the substance of the faith is not touched by them. However, there were schisms in the full meaning of the word already during the earliest periods of Christianity. Back even to apostolic times, again and again we find groups of Christians who for liturgical, theological, or national reasons separated themselves from the universal Church.

The main stage for these schisms during the first thousand years was the East, the region of the intellectual development of that age. It was there that the question of the relationship between the humanity and the divinity of Christ was first raised. As Christianity came to be more than a mere personal experience immediately felt and lived, as it began to think through the tenets of its faith, questions arose: Who was Christ? Was He God? Was He man? Was He God only, or man only? Or both together?

One answer said: He was a man in whom dwelt the second person of God, the eternal logos, but only as the soul dwelled in the human body. Therefore, Mary was not to be called Mother of God, only mother of Christ. Nestorius, Patriarch of Constantinople, adopted this concept. It was condemned under the name Nestorianism by the Third Ecumenical Council of Ephesus in 431, and thereby the truth of the dual nature in one divine person of Christ was established as the doctrine of the universal Church. The Persian Christians rebelled against this decision of the council and accepted Nestorianism as their official doctrine. By this act they separated themselves from the universal Church. Today, the Nestorians count only about 85,000 believers.

But the questions about Christ had not been laid to rest. Now that it had been established that the Redeemer of the human race was not a mere man, simply used by the triune God for the fulfillment of His plan of salvation, but a unique God-Man, *one* person who simultaneously was both God *and* man, another question arose: What was the precise *nature* of this God-Man? Was it divine or human, or both? Here, too, the various theological schools of thought did not all give the same answer.

Some taught that only the divine nature was operative in Christ; the divine nature had, as it were, swallowed up His human nature, absorbed it.

Against this concept, the Fourth Ecumenical Council of Chalcedon (near Constantinople) took its stand in 451. It branded Monophysitism, the one-nature doctrine (from the Greek *mono+physis*=one nature), as a heresy, and proclaimed it as orthodox doctrine that both natures, the divine and the human, were present in Christ "undivided and unadulterated."

Some countries rejected the decrees of this council. But, as the Nestorians twenty years before, they also found themselves in opposition to the Roman Empire. These countries were: Egypt, Syria, somewhat later Armenia, and finally, in the wake of Egypt, Ethiopia, whose Church was an offspring of the Egyptian Church. In the period following, these Churches were referred to as Monophysite Churches. However, this expression is not quite correct, for these Churches did not teach the doctrine of the one nature (which alone would justify this term); they in fact rejected this doctrine, just as the Council of Chalcedon had rejected it. They also rejected the Council's formulations, however, insisting that these formulations reverted back to Nestorianism. Because of this rejection of the Fourth Ecumenical Council, rigidly maintained to the present day, these groups no longer belong to the universal Church.

Monophysite Christians are not very numerous today. They are divided into: (1) *Copts*[1] (approximately three million). Their form of Christianity follows the Alexandrian rite. (2) *Ethiopians* (approximately six million), sometimes also but erroneously called Copts. They, too, follow the Alexandrian rite. (3) *Syrians,* also called Jacobites after Jacob Baradai who reorganized them in the sixth century (about 150,000). Added to them should be some 800,000 Jacobites scattered along the Malabar coast of India, also referred to as Thomas Christians; they follow the West-Syrian or Antioch rite. (4) *Armenians* (approximately three and a half million), sometimes also called Gregorians after the "Apostle of Armenia," Gregor the Illuminator; they follow the Armenian rite.

An offshoot of Monophysitism was Monothelitism. It taught only *one will* in Christ, but it has no adherents today.

The third great schism is the so-called Eastern Schism

---

1. Copts: the word is a European form of the Arabic "Kibit" which is derived from the Greek word for Egyptians.

of 1054. It was there that the unity between the Rome of the West and Constantinople, the "Rome of the East," broke visibly apart. This time, the reason was not the acceptance or rejection of the decisions of a council, but an alienation between the Eastern and Western parts of the Roman Empire—an estrangement which had been long in the making. In the year 1054 this alienation, which had already lasted over some centuries because of divergent concepts of the papacy and of the Church, was made official by a legal act: The papal delegate, Cardinal Umberto, deposited on the altar of the church Hagia Sophia in Constantinople the bull of excommunication against Michael Cerularius, Patriarch of Constantinople "and his adherents." Cerularius replied with the excommunication of Umberto. In spite of various attempts on both sides to heal this schism, it has not been overcome to this day. Ever since 1054, the terms "Catholic" ("all-embracing") and "Orthodox" ("of the true faith") both of which the West and the East originally had in common, were increasingly used to denote separateness. The West now calls itself Catholic, the East Orthodox.

Unlike the Catholic Church, the Orthodox Church is not centrally governed; it is ruled instead by the principle of collegiality. All major Churches are independently governed, mostly along national lines. Only smaller Churches exist in a relationship of dependence on larger ones. Thus there are the Greek-Orthodox, Russian-Orthodox, Rumanian-Orthodox Churches. Sometimes the term Greek-Orthodox is used to denote the Orthodox Church as a whole because it received its characteristic qualities from Greek Byzantium. The liturgical rite which is followed uniformly by all Orthodox national Churches also is

Byzantine. Corresponding to the individual cult languages, there are Byzantine-Greek, Byzantine-Slavonic (for Russians, Serbs, Bulgars), Byzantine-Rumanian, Byzantine-Hungarian cults, and so on. The rite of the Orthodox who live in areas of the Arabic cult-language is called Melchite. Melchite (meaning a supporter of the emperor at Byzantium) was the name given in Monophysite countries to the Christians who remained faithful to the Orthodox beliefs. The word has its root in the Syrian word *malko*—king. The number of all Orthodox Christians is approximately 200 million.

An entirely different history is that of the Christians who are settled along the Malabar coast of India. There, schisms, reunions, changes of rites, and conversions to a variety of other Christian confessions followed each other in bewildering succession. Today one can find represented among the roughly one and a half million Christians in Malabar, almost all denominations and rites of the East and the West.

In the course of the centuries, Rome attempted to restore the original unity with the various Eastern Churches. It tried a system of "Unions," so-called—a method of approach considered especially suited to the Orthodox—but one that has by no means had consistent success.

The principle underlying these unions was to permit the Orthodox to retain their Eastern characteristics, provided they recognized the jurisdictional primacy of the pope. In the practical work of these unions, however, this principle has never been really applied. Although the Uniates do recognize the pope as the supreme pontiff, they have only partially been able to retain their Eastern individualities. Many Western customs intrinsically foreign to them have been introduced into their forms of Christianity. Their piety is influenced almost exclusively by Western ideals. Eastern theology is nowhere being taught (except as a minor historical discipline). Nearly the entire monastic ideal is formed after Western examples. Their clerics are being educated like Latin clerics, but as something of a special bonus they are permitted to learn their inherited rite; yet even that, almost without exception, is colored, more or less strongly, by Roman features. The problems arising from Eastern ecclesiastical law are extremely complicated; to this day no solution has been found that is satisfactory to all concerned.

These instances of Latinization are all the more regretable because *in principle* the government of the Roman Church has always recognized the juridical equality of the Eastern individuality. Pope Benedict XV once said: "Even though some, out of an exaggerated desire for unity and concord, and out of ignorance of the Orientals and their individuality have attempted to change their sacred rites and to make them more like the Latin, the Roman popes, our predecessors, have with all their power resisted such efforts as best they could."

Unfortunately, this true catholicity has not yet become the common property of all Christians in the Western Church.

A contributing factor, as we shall see, was the fact that the several unions established between Rome and the Eastern Churches were never able to embrace more than small groups of Christians. Faced with the practical preponderance of the Roman sister-Church, an influence the more noticeable the more charity was lacking, feelings of inferiority developed easily among the Eastern members, to the point that they were eager and willing to accept Latinization.

These unions cover a span of nearly 800 years. The first one was formed about the time of the Crusades, the last one at the beginning of our century. Let us now take a closer look at them.

The Various "Uniate" Churches

1. The Chaldaeans

The first attempts at union occurred among the Nestorians in the sixteenth century. Those who converted to Catholicism could no longer be identified with the name of the heretical Nestorians. So the name Chaldaeans was chosen for them. Today they comprise a community of about 200,000 believers, all of whom are settled in Iraq, Iran, and Syria. Their liturgical practices are heavily Latinized. Their head bears the title Patriarch of Babylon; his election must be confirmed by the pope. The current bearer of this title is Mar Paul II. He resides in Baghdad. East Syrian is used as the liturgical language. The rite itself is called East-Syrian or Persian.

2. The Malabar Christians

The so-called Thomas Christians along the Malabar coast of India, who originally were dependent on the Nestorian patriarch, were first united with Rome in the sixteenth century by the Portuguese. In 1599 began the ill-famed Synod of Djampore which was dominated by the Portuguese who were bent on the forcible Latinization of the Thomas Christians. It led to mass apostasy from

Rome, a schism which reached its climax in 1652. After that, some of the groups that had fallen away returned again to communion with Rome. The rest, however, did not return to Nestorianism, but put themselves instead under the jurisdiction of the Jacobite patriarch. Those united with Rome are now called Malabar Christians. Today they number about a million adherents. Their highest-ranking bishop is the Metropolitan of Ernakulam. His authority equals that of an archbishop in the Latin Church. Latinization is very conspicuous in the Malabar rite. Most ceremonies follow the Roman ritual, and even the vestments are Roman. However, there are efforts underway to restore to the East-Syrian rite its original form. The ecclesiastic language is East-Syrian; but Malayalam, the vernacular, is also used.

3. *The Copts*

Among the Copts, who are descendants of the ancient Egyptians, attempts at union reach back to the seventeenth century. But for long these efforts met with little success. Not until 1895 was it possible for them to establish a hierarchy of their own. The Coptic community comprises today about 80,000 people. Their spiritual head is the Patriarch of Alexandria. He bears the same title as the head of the Coptic branch that is not in communion with Rome. The present uniate patriarch is Amba Stephanos (Sydaruss). Both Coptic and Arabic are used as liturgical languages.

4. *The Ethiopians*

In the seventeenth century there were some short-lived attempts at union in Ethiopia, but because of the strong tendencies towards Latinization, they had no success. It was not until the nineteenth century that the idea of union with Rome could gain ground again. The number of faithful today is not great: some 40,000. The highest-ranking bishop is the Apostolic Exarch of Ethiopia who resides in Addis-Ababa. The liturgical language is Gheez, the classical language of the Ethiopians.

5. *The Syrians*

Union efforts with the Syrians were begun in the sixteenth century. In the seventeenth century some small progress was made, and since 1783 there has continuously been a uniate Syrian patriarch. His title, like that of his non-uniate colleague, is Patriarch of Antioch. At the present time this office is held by Mar Gabriel I (Tappuni). He has been a Roman cardinal since 1935. The uniate Syrians form a community of some 100,000 faithful. The liturgical languages are West-Syrian and Arabic.

6. *The Malankara Catholics*

Among the Jacobites of the Malabar coast of India (see the Malabar Christians above), there also developed a movement for union with Rome. In 1930 two of their bishops joined Rome, and this movement has been sustained to the present day. These Christians are called Malankara Catholics. Their number is in the neighborhood of 90,000 and is still growing. Their spiritual head presently is Mar Gregorius, Metropolitan and Archbishop of Trivandrum. West-Syrian and Malayalam are both used as liturgical languages.

7. The Maronites

Originally, the Maronites belonged to the Syrian Church. Why they broke away from it and why they started a community of their own, gathered around the monastery of St. Maron in Lebanon, lies buried in the dark ages of history. Western scholars assume that they had given way to Monothelitism, and for this reason separated themselves from the Syrian Church. Maronites themselves deny this and insist on having maintained full union with Rome at all times. At any rate, there are in existence two unquestionable sources which attest to the *re*union of the Maronites with Rome, which in all probability took place in the year 1181. The Maronites are the only Eastern community which is totally united with Rome. Today they have about half a million members, who live mostly in Lebanon. The president of the State of Lebanon always is a Maronite. The current head of the Church is Msgr. Paul Peter Meuschi, Patriarch of Antioch. Like the Malabar Church, the Maronite Church also is strictly Latinized, and Roman vestments have taken the place of Syrian vestments. For an observer not conversant with details, a Maronite Low Mass is indistinguishable from a Roman Mass. Arabic and West-Syrian serve as liturgical languages.

8. The Armenians

The first union with the Armenians was concluded in the year 1198. Because it was a matter of political expediency, however, it came to an end again in 1375. In the eighteenth century attempts at union were revived, and today there are a little more than 100,000 uniate Armenians. Their spiritual head is Gregor Petrus XV (Agadschaniàn),

Patriarch of Sis in Kilikis. The patriarch, who himself uses the Italian spelling of his name, Agagianian, was made a Cardinal in 1946. His residence is Beirut. Since 1958 he also heads the Congregation of Missions, a fact which may give rise to the hope that the Eastern rites, which are especially suited to the Oriental peoples and their mentality, will in the future be taken into consideration in the work of the missions among the Oriental pagans.

9. *The Byzantine Rite*

Negotiations for union with the Orthodox Church have taken place time and again. They have always been fruitless, as far as the Orthodox Church as a body is concerned. Efforts to induce individual national Churches, dioceses, or individuals to be reunited with Rome have had somewhat better success. Chronologically listed, the following groups are involved:

(a) 1595: Union at Brest-Litowsk with the Ruthenians (today called Ukrainians) of Poland-Lithuania, two countries which then lived in political union. After the divisions of Poland, the union with Rome was suppressed in those parts that had fallen to Russia; it continued to exist only in the parts that had been ceded to Austria. Under Empress Maria Theresa, the government in Vienna designated the Orthodox uniates as "Greek-Orthodox" under the leadership of the Metropolitan of Lemberg. When Poland was restored in 1920, a new period of suffering began for the Ukrainians who came under Polish domination; it reached its height in 1945 when the new Soviet government declared the uniate Church as simply non-existent. Numerically strong groups of uniate exiles have sprung up in Western Europe and especially on the American continent. For the Ukrainian uniates living in Germany a new archbishopric was recently created in Munich. Before World War II, the uniate Ukrainians counted approximately 5 million; they are still the largest group today.

(b) Seventeenth century: Union with a group of Serbs who had emigrated to Croatia. Today they form the "Greek-Catholic" diocese of Kriz with 55,000 members.

(c) 1697-1700: Union with the Rumanians of Transylvania. In today's Rumania this Church exists only in hiding. Before the war it had a million and a half members.

(d) Eighteenth century: Union attempts with the Melchites. Partial union still exists. Their head is Maximos IV, Patriarch of Antioch, Alexandria, and Jerusalem. Approximately 250,000 faithful.

(e) Nineteenth century: Union attempts with the Greeks of Asia Minor. Partial union still in existence. Athens Eparchy: about 2000 communicants; Constantinople Eparchy: about 1000.

(f) Nineteenth century: Union attempts with the Bulgarians of Constantinople, Thracia, and Macedonia. Initially great successes but followed by reversals. Before the war, the uniate Apostolic Administration of Bulgaria comprised 7000 faithful.

(g) Beginning of the twentieth century: Union attempts in Russia but with very little success; then suppressed by the Soviets. Efforts among several Russian émigré groups practically without success. Approximately 1000 faithful.

General View of the Situation Today

Looking over the work of these unions as a whole, we must admit that the main goal, the union of the Eastern Churches with the Roman Church, has not been achieved.

Of approximately 250 million Orthodox, only about ten million are united with Rome. The blame for this failure, as already indicated, must to a great extent be laid to the lack of readiness on the Catholic side to grant equality to the legitimate individualities of the uniates. This unwillingness has deepened the historically rooted contrasts between East and West. "Catholic" came to be identified with "Western," and this prevented the greater part of the Orthodox from entering into communion with Rome. The many instances of Latinization and denials of their rights, to which the uniates succumbed, served as a warning to those not in union with Rome. They saw in these examples a preview of what might be in store for them if they decided for union. And so, the union work which was originally intended as a bridge between Rome and the East, achieved precisely the opposite effect: it widened the existing gulf even more. The non-Roman Christians of the East became passionate opponents of union and fought it wherever they saw an opportunity to do so. The name "uniates" by which those Christians who had united with Rome were known, became a phrase of contempt for those who were looked upon as neither Catholic nor Orthodox, neither Eastern nor Western, neither fish nor flesh.

Today, the old style union efforts are fading away in the Roman Church. The "New Union Work," so-called, is doing everything possible to let the Christians of the East be indeed Easterners.

The tendencies inspired by the new ecumenical spirit go even further. Ecumenical thinking, in principle, leads more and more in the direction of concentrating not so much on group-union and individual conversions but rather on mutual rapprochement of the Western and Eastern Churches, eliminating all subjective polemics and all power plays. This is the way which Pope John XXIII advocated: *riavvicinamento* (rapprochement), *riaccosta-mento* (cooperation), *riunione perfetta* (perfect unity).

Prospects

Even though it must be said that the road of the various unions of the past cannot lead to the end goal "that all may be one," it would nonetheless be wrong to look with disdain on the uniates as though they were but the victims of an illusion. These Churches have had and still have an almost superhumanly difficult task to fulfill: to awaken understanding and sympathy in the Western Church for the Christianity of the East. Without the existence of the uniates, this consciousness would perhaps never have come to life; without them the realization could perhaps never have dawned what psychological difficulties are involved when several Churches, united with each other, intend to live together on a somewhat tolerable foundation. The uniate Churches of the East have not made their sacrifice in vain; they have laid it on the altar of a future reunion, the pioneers of which they have become in the process of clearing away many obstacles on the road. Even though they do not point to the ideal road we can walk together, they at least show us clearly which way *not* to use. A future ecumenical theology which will concern itself with the problems of the East, will not be able to bypass the experience of the uniate Churches; on many points, as for example on the doctrine of the Church itself, they will have to build on what the uniates have begun.

Finally, the uniates have created in the Roman Church a new awareness of the breadth of its catholicity. For that alone they deserve our deepest gratitude. "Latin" and "Catholic" can now no longer be confused. The new understanding and demarcation of concepts we gained through them has prepared the ground on which a fruitful meeting of Church with Church can take place. The real importance of the uniates for interconfessional relations will perhaps only be recognized in retrospect, centuries from now.

5

Margot Hiemerer | CARDINAL NEWMAN
AND THE UNITY
OF THE CHURCH

THE DECISION OF Pope John XXIII to call an ecumenical council has awakened in the Catholic Church more strongly than ever before the hope for the reunification of divided Christianity. Even though this council can not yet be one of union—the minds of men on either side are as yet not prepared for that—it nonetheless cannot help furthering, even though indirectly, the cause of ecumenism. At this moment, when ecumenical concerns have become more and more urgent, we look around for men to help us in the task of overcoming in charity our divisions in matters of faith.

The English cardinal, John Henry Newman, is recognized today as one of the greatest ecumenical figures in whose personal struggle for the truth is reflected the struggle of all Christians for reunion. His main works from both his Catholic and his Anglican periods are known all over the world, and one cannot escape the feeling that they were written precisely for our present time. Especially is this true in their pertinence to ecumenical work. Newman's entire life revolved around the search for the one, catholic, and apostolic Church.

Newman and the Church of England

John Henry Newman was born February 24, 1801, in London. His father was a London banker who came from the county of Cambridge. His mother was of French Huguenot stock; her family had fled from France to England after the revocation of the Edict of Nantes. In contrast to her husband, she was a deeply religious person and brought up her children from their earliest years in reverence for the word of God. In Henry, the sober, analytical mind of the father was combined with the tenderness, the sympathetic understanding and depth of feeling he had inherited from his mother. The combination of these elements showed itself in that particular intellectual sensibility which enabled him to do justice to all sides of a subject, all the facts of a case, seeing in each what was true and yet recognizing the limits of these truths.

Early in his youth something happened to Newman which he called his "conversion." He experienced within himself the certainty that there is a God who speaks to us through our conscience and on whom our salvation depends. The disturbing aspect of this breakthrough of God into the very being of Newman was God's overwhelming reality. This interior conversion Newman considered as even more certain than the possession of his hands and feet. The belief in this reality of God detached him even more from the things of his environment and confirmed in him the mistrust in the reality of the world of material appearances. This personal experience of salvation was so strong in Newman that for a time he seemed to forget about the salvation of other men. However, his reflection upon himself was soon widened again by a new study of the doctrine of the faith and by new thoughts on the community of the Church. Thus, there are always two forces which intellectually propel Newman's work: the dialogue between his own person and God, the Creator; and the Church. Neither of these impulses can be overlooked if Newman is to be rightly understood.

In 1817 Newman entered Trinity College at Oxford. In order to appreciate Newman, one has to know something of the atmosphere of Oxford. Whatever life may have taught Newman, it never could erase the characteristics which the famous colleges of Oxford—Trinity and Oriel— gave him. There the goal of education was not the accumulation of knowledge, as he himself emphasized, but the formation of the intellect. Thus Newman's intellect was formed at Oxford not only by knowledge imparted but even more by the atmosphere of erudition and scholarship blended with astuteness which seizes every one who lives in Oxford.

In 1820 he decided to stay at the university to study theology. He was influenced in this decision chiefly by two Anglican theologians. They not only taught him to think independently but also to order his thoughts and to express them with precision. From then on he accepted the idea that the Christian Church is a divine institution and a visible, corporate body, independent of the state and endowed with rights, privileges, and authority of its own.

Of even greater importance for Newman was the friendship with a few men who together fought with all their powers for the purification of the Anglican Church in order to preserve it as the successor to the ancient Church. The Anglican Church was at that time in a sad state of affairs.

Perhaps in no other institution have the English given such an obvious proof of their predilection for compromise than in their official state Church. It is certainly possible to say that the official forms, ceremonies, and doctrines of the Church of England are not based on a God-given reality but rather on an arbitrary compromise.

The Creed, as it is formulated in the thirty-ninth article of the Anglican Church, is a composite of parts of Catholicism, Lutheranism, Calvinism, and Zwinglianism. Luther, Calvin, Zwingli were all opponents of Rome, but they also were opponents of one another. Still it is correct to say that the structure of the Anglican Church is a synthesis of all these variations of Protestantism with a strong admixture of Catholicism. The doctrine of the Anglican Church is the result of the successive influences of King Henry VIII, who in 1531 decreed the separation of the English Church from Rome and thereby founded his own "Church of England," of the cabinet ministers of his son, Edward V, of his daughters Mary and Elizabeth I, of the Puritans, of the Methodists of the eighteenth century, and of the liberals.

The Anglican Church has a hierarchy in the medieval style which occupies a position of eminence in social life and also exerts political influence. It can look back on a line of theologians, especially in the seventeenth century, who possessed great learning and took pride in their approach to the practices of the early Church.

This English Church has always been subservient to the secular power. It always looked at papal power with uneasiness and aversion. In the nineteenth century, the Anglican Church was represented by three strong groups. In each of these was embodied one of the three religious principles which from the beginning on, in one form or another, were prominent in the religious history of England, namely, the Catholic, the Protestant, and the skeptical element. The first is expressed in the High Church, which stands closest to Catholicism. The Protestant principle is represented by the "Evangelicals," the moving element of the Bible societies all over the world. The skeptical principle finds its representation in the liberal faction. Besides these, there was an even larger group which provided the equilibrium and the unifying bond for the whole: the political party of the conservatives, the Tory party. Tory principles and slogans have more of a political, even though ecclesiastical-political, than theological nature. The Tories were and are champions of a state Church, much more concerned with the fact that there should exist a national Church than with what its doctrines are. They look with suspicion on all theology and theological factions, especially the three here mentioned.

Three divisions of the Anglican Church of the nineteenth century need some further explanation because they continue into the present time, namely, the High Church, the Low Church, and the Broad Church. By the term Broad Church is meant, by-and-large, the liberal, less Church-directed group. But High Church and Low Church cannot be so readily comprehended. The High Church is the conservative wing of the Anglican Church. Although it most closely represents the essence of the Anglican Church, it cannot simply be equated with the Anglican Church as a whole. The High Church is only one segment within the Anglican Church. It is that group which attaches great importance to the privileges and authority of the Church; in the nineteenth century however, it was not so much concerned with the invisible resources of the Church than with the prerogatives and attributes which it possesses as a corporate institution. The High Church emphasizes its hierarchical constitution, its continuity with the Church of early Christianity, and the early Middle Ages. Since about 1860, it attached itself even more than before to the cult and liturgy of the ancient Church.

In the Low Church, dogmatic questions also remain in the background. In the center of interest stands the personal sanctification of the individual. The goal of Christian formation in the Low Church is the cultivation of a practical, individual piety, and the Low Church has to its credit great efforts to popularize the Bible.

At the end of the eighteenth century, the liberal tendencies of the official state Church spread wider and wider. A new beginning was urgently needed in the Church because the supernatural element was being increasingly neglected. Doctrine was nowhere to be found. In Manchester, the Lord's Supper was celebrated only every three months. Patens that had been used in Church services could be found in inns and bars, and chalices formerly used at Mass found their way to the tables of the rich. The prevailing sentiment of the day, the spirit of the time, was directed against Christianity. The Gospel, with its contradiction of the world's wisdom, was rejected. What the world decries as foolishness is in reality the instinctive faith of the Christian in a wisdom greater than his own. The Gospel itself says as much. But the Anglican Church had forgotten that.

In Oxford, a circle of theologians under the spiritual leadership of Newman had come to see that the ideas of the Reformation were no longer capable of rescuing the

Church from this danger, and that, if the Church was to be saved, a second reformation was needed. The efforts of these men to bring about a second reformation for the Church of England are known in history under the name of the Oxford Movement. The aim of this movement was the renewal of the Church, the reawakening of the original Christian tradition in the face of the liberalizing state Church. Newman believed that this liberalism had to be checked in the first place by means of a stronger intellectual defense of Christianity, and secondly (which was even more important to him) by strengthening the Church in its substance. For the Church is the protector of dogma. Within three years the movement became a power in Oxford and in the country. Still, nobody suspected where Newman and his friends would be led by all this just a few short years later.

In the summer of 1845 a great number of Newman's friends from the Oxford Movement entered the Catholic Church. Before that, Newman himself had already withdrawn from Oxford because of his own intention to take the same step. The unity of the movement was thus broken and its purpose obscured. After Newman left Oxford, the liberals again obtained the upper hand, and with this the Oxford Movement soon lost its significance. Newman became a Catholic in October, 1845. This year was probably the most decisive period in Newman's life, as he, the celebrated Oxford theologian and preacher, joined the Catholic Church.

Newman the Anglican, and the Unity of the Church

As we inquire into Newman's concept of the Church, it must first of all be noted that he apparently went through various phases. One thing, however, remains permanent in both Newman the Anglican and Newman the Catholic: The Church as a living reality. Unfolding in history and in the present, the Church is the reality of God's revelation in Jesus Christ. In speaking of the Church, therefore, we are dealing with a supernatural reality which manifests itself in this world—in the visible Church. The thought that the Church is a historical reality occurred to Newman time and again in his study of the time of the Fathers. With its sacraments, its doctrine, and its hierarchy, the Church is inserted into the world by God. In speaking of the Church as a reality, he means that it is more than a complex of propositions and dogmas, external precepts and customs; more also than the sum of its individual members. It exists as a creation of God which antedates the individuals in it.

In Newman's view, the Church is inextricably joined to the incarnation of Jesus Christ. It is, in his own words, "the Christ among us." It lives through and in Christ, transmitting and representing His life in word and sacrament. There is no way to Christ without the Church, as it has evolved in history. It secures salvation for men; it offers to the individual the possibility to take hold of his salvation; it guarantees him God's redeeming acceptance —and it thereby restores the existential reality of man, disordered by sin, to the original relationship between creature and Creator. Yet, this is not to imply that Newman sees the Church exclusively from the point of view of man. On the contrary, he sees it as an institution introduced into history by God. Since the Church is thus an objective entity, it is possible for it to secure salvation for the individual who is part of it. Fundamental for this concept of the Church, which is well-founded in the New

Testament, is Newman's acceptance of man as essentially a creature given to error. Only in God is there absolute truth, and this truth means salvation for the man who accepts it. God's truth has been revealed to man in the person of Christ and, after His ascension, through the Church.

But wherein does the unity of the Church consist? The basis for the unity of the Church is not found in the decisions of the Councils, not in the subjective faith of the individual, not even in the commonly professed Creed—all these are mere external factors. The essential foundation for the unity of the Church is the one unchanging and complete reality: God. In the Church, those who follow Christ are united by a visible bond into one body. Through the sacrament of Baptism, the faithful are incorporated into this already existing body. Christ has secured the unity of the Church by appointing holders of spiritual offices. These spiritual offices are the bond which merges the entire body of Christendom into one union. Newman establishes this point in great detail and exclusively from Holy Scripture. It must be specifically noted here that he owes his faith in the Church, in its office and its sacraments, not to Roman Catholic doctrine, but he arrived at his conclusions through his own study of Holy Scripture and of the traditions familiar to him.

When Christ founded the Church, he established its unity in the office of Peter. Newman comments on Matt. 16:18:

> In St. Peter, who is there made the rock on which the Church is founded, we see, as in a type, its unity, stability, and permanence.[1]

---

1. *Parochial and Plain Sermons*, Vol. 7, London, 1868, 231.

Peter and the other Apostles appointed successors who became the witnesses of a living tradition.

The unity with which Christ endowed the Church, however, is not an automatic uniformity; it depends on the "realization" of the faith by the individual believer. In fact, the unity of the Church threatens to become a mere appearance of unity, unless the Christians in the world live together here on earth in a visible society, . . . "not as a confused, unconnected multitude, but united and organized one with another, by an established order, so as evidently to appear and to act as one." [2]

This conviction also came to Newman from Holy Scripture. Whenever Holy Scripture speaks of unity, it means an *active* unity which is to determine the practical life of the Christian here on earth—not merely a desire, an affirmation of unity side by side with actual disunity and schism. We Christians, says Newman, can never be of one heart and mind, unless obedience to the Church is part of our existence.

With this conviction Newman now had to ask himself where the reality of the Church and the requirements of unity were most completely fulfilled. As an Anglican, he naturally looked for them in his Anglican community and found them in the great Catholic-oriented theologians of the seventeenth century: Butler, Andrews, and Laud. He and his friends in the Oxford Movement believed that the Anglican Church merely had to take seriously its own principles and return to its own tradition in order to be truly Catholic and Apostolic. Basing his theory on the liturgy of the Book of Common Prayer, the generally ac-

---

2. *Ibid.* p. 234.

cepted English prayer book, he wanted to give a new theology to the Anglican Church aimed at cleansing it from the influence of the Reformers of the sixteenth century. At the same time, however, he was scandalized by the practices of the Roman Catholic Church, as he had come to know it in England and on the Continent. On his journey to Italy he found the Catholic Church, as he wrote later, so corrupted he could have wept, and until the year 1843 he still clung to the opinion that the Roman Church was the anti-Christ possessed by the Devil.

So Newman became the representative of the *via media* theory. According to this thinking, the Anglican Church occupied a middle ground between Romanism (Roman Catholicism) and Protestantism as commonly practised at the time. In his book *The Prophetic Office of the Church* (1837) the *via media* theory is at length developed. However, this theory is not to be considered a mere lame compromise lacking in principles, a coming to terms with things objected to; it is indicative of the efforts on his part to do justice to the various points of view of a problem, a decision, or an event, in order to see the whole, and thereby the truth. The Anglican Church, as it appeared to Newman, seemed to hold the right balance between Romanism and Protestantism, and for this reason appeared to be the ideal rallying point for all Churches.

As already indicated, Newman at that time had no sympathy at all for Rome. As late as 1842, only two years before his conversion, he displayed a decidedly uncompromising attitude toward Rome. The gloomy impressions he gained during his Italian journey on the state of affairs of the ecclesiastical and religious life actually left him with the fear that Christianity might be rapidly approaching its doom. One Sunday morning he writes from Italy:

> I think of St. Mary's and Littlemore. We do
> not know how great our privileges are. All
> the quiet and calm connected with our serv-
> ices is so beautiful in memory, and so sooth-
> ing, after the sight of that most exciting reli-
> gion which is around me—statues of the Ma-
> donna and the Saints in the streets . . .[3]

Nevertheless, his judgment remains balanced. He sees
light as well as darkness:

> What mingled feelings come upon one—you
> are in the place of martyrdom and burial of
> apostles and saints; you have about you the
> buildings and the sights they saw, and you
> are in the city to which England owes the
> blessing of the gospel. But then, on the other
> hand, the superstitions, or rather, what is far
> worse, the solemn reception of them as an
> essential part of Christianity. But then, again,
> the extreme beauty and costliness of the
> churches; and then, on the contrary, the
> knowledge that the most famous was built
> (in part) by the sale of indulgences. Really
> this is a cruel place.[4]

At this time, Newman makes a significant distinction
between "Roman" and "Catholic":

> As to the *Roman* Catholic system, I have ever

---

3. *Letters and Correspondence of J. H. Newman*, Vol. 1, London,
1891, p. 338.
4. *Ibid.*, p. 325.

> detested it so much that I cannot detest it more by seeing it; but to the Catholic system I am more attached than ever, and quite love the little monks (seminarists) of Rome; they look so innocent and bright, poor boys! . . . I fear that there are very grave and far-spreading scandals among the Italian priest-hood, and there is mummery in abundance; yet there is a deep substratum of true Christianity . . .[5]

And in the *Via media* one can read:

> In Romanism there are some things absolutely good, some things only just tainted and sullied, some things corrupted, and some things in themselves sinful; but the system itself so-called must be viewed as a whole.[6]

From all this, one can now understand Newman's reasoning which made him conclude that he had to remain in the Anglican Church. He enumerates seven reasons:

1. The experience of a religious conversion time and again renewed, by which a religious man is mysteriously and invisibly made over.

2. In the Church of England God had granted him more grace and strength for a new life than he knew how to use.

3. The actual experience of Divine guidance and the experience of more or less miraculous providential happenings.

4. The unmistakable proof of prayers heard.

5. *Ibid.*, p. 378.
6. *The Via Media of the Anglican Church,* Vol. 1, London, 1877, p. 84.

5. Personal experiences in connection with the liturgical and sacramental life of the Church.

6. The manifestation of the tangible presence of Christ at deathbeds:

> May we not reverently hope that Almighty God does sometimes vouchsafe to show bystanders then, that our Church, in spite of its manifold disorders, is a safe Church to die in?[7]

7. The mark of a holy life.

Now, how did Newman, starting from the theology of the *via media,* conceive the reunification of the separated Christians? It was the great hope of Newman, the Anglican, that the reunification might be made possible by a reform *on both sides.* The task, as he saw it, was to reform those things in both Churches which, because of the sinfulness of their members, were in need of reformation. On the Anglican side, the need for reform lay especially in the problem of freeing the Church from its links to the state and from its humanist-liberal tendencies. At that time Newman advocated on principle a corporate union between the Anglican and the Catholic Church. He saw the solution of the problem in a return of the entire Anglican Church, as a body, to Rome. This return was not to be the decision of individuals only; that, he thought, would be in contradiction to the corporate spirit of Catholicism. He wrote to Father Faber in September 1843:

> Is it not the ordinary way of Providence, both

---

7. *Sermons Bearing on Subjects of the Day,* London, 1869, p. 355.

> as a precept and a mercy, that men should not
> make great changes by themselves, or on pri-
> vate judgment, but should change with the
> body in which they find themselves, or at least
> in company.[8]

Newman therefore censored most sharply all Catholic attempts to make individual converts among the Anglicans
and, for the same reason, he also found himself unable
to join any of the reunification movements in which Catholics also were members.

All this shows that Newman believed in the Anglican
community as in a Church. This was his concern also in
regard to the Oxford Movement, namely, that it might
arouse the people's sympathies for Rome. One must never
forget that against the liberal process of disintegration
Newman was fighting for the unity of his Church:

> Did we go over to the Roman Catholics, we
> should be fomenting divisions among our-
> selves, which would be a prima facie case
> against us. . . . Besides, there are the Apos-
> tle's injunctions against disorder.[9]

Nothing seemed to him so obstructive in relation to unification than proselytizing. In June, 1841, he wrote to a
Catholic: "If your friends wish to put a gulf between
them and us, let them make converts." (Quoted by Newman himself in the *Apologia Pro Vita Sua.*)

---

8. *Correspondence of J. H. Card. Newman with John Keble and Others*
(1839–1845), London, 1917, p. 253.
9. *Via Media,* Vol. 2, p. 98.

Newman the Catholic, and the Unity of the Church

In October 1845, Newman became a Catholic. How was this possible in so quiet a man, a man so eminently gifted with extraordinary balance in his thinking and so pronounced in his dispassionate approach?

At the end of 1839, the *via media* theory had collapsed. Time and again before his conversion, Newman had attempted to find a positive foundation for the Anglican Church: some proof that it was indeed Revelation realized. But his hope in the Anglican Church sank more and more. Of course, the question of truth stood for Newman always in the foreground. He was convinced that man stands under the truth, not above it, and that he was therefore bound in conscience to respect and preserve the truth. On September 25, 1843, he preached a farewell sermon to his Anglican friends. He knew now that he had been brought up in a system outside the truth, and he concluded:

> Surely the *continuance* of a person, who wishes to go right, in a wrong system, and not his *giving it up,* would be that which militated against the objectiveness of Truth, leading, as it would, to the suspicion, that one thing and another were equally pleasing to our Maker, where men were sincere.[10]

Newman may indeed be called the theologian of conscience. He was convinced that a man must follow his conscience, even when erring, as long as no doubt arose in him that he might be in error. Now, such a doubt existed

10. *Apologia Pro Vita Sua,* London, 1902, p. 206.

in Newman at that time, and it was for this reason that he considered it his duty to search for the rational causes for his inner inclination and presentiment. This meant for him that he had to hold himself open to the possible truth of Rome, and to determine whether or not his objections against Rome were indeed objective, or whether they existed only subjectively, perhaps only in his prejudices. Since he did not feel himself bound any longer to the Anglican Church which had thus far been his authority, because it no longer offered to his conscience any rational argument which would have commanded acceptance, he now looked for these rational arguments in the only external authority left to him: the history of the Church. And there he found that the truth lay in Rome.

His turning toward Rome did not constitute a substantial personal change; he merely was prompted by the realization that the Churches actually in existence proved in reality to be different from what he had conceived. The more he studied the history of the early Church and the theology of the Church Fathers, the more irresistible became his conviction that the Church of Rome alone represented the organic continuity of the early Church. Time and again he admits that his studies of the Church Fathers and of the history of the ancient Church were the sole intellectual reasons for his alienation from Anglicanism and his turning to Roman Catholicism. It was through these studies that he saw the essential sameness of the Catholic Church of his own time and the Church of the first centuries. On his way to Catholicism, Newman then freed himself from his earlier opinion that only the Church of the beginning, not the whole of Church history, consti-

tuted the crucial and original historical reality. Now he
saw in the entirety of Church history the fulness of the
Church's existence. If he accepted the ancient councils,
then he also had to accept the Council of Trent, for what
was at stake in both instances was the same principle.

In 1844, looking back to the year 1839, Newman referred in various letters in his voluminous correspondence
to the conviction which over the past four years had ma-
tured in his mind—that the Anglican Church did not stand
on the side of truth. He describes how in the course of
his regular reading he was led to the Monophysite controversy and to the Council of Chalcedon and St. Leo's
work. He clearly saw the position of the Novatians, the
Arians, the Donatists, Nestorians, and Monophysites, and,
reflected in them, he saw the problems of his own day in
all their variants. He saw the position of the Church of
Rome represented in the stern, uncompromising, even
imperious but always decisive, attitude of the saints of
the ancient Church: Ignatius of Antioch, Cyprian, Athanasius, Augustine, and Leo. "In a word," he says in one of
these letters, "I found a complete and wonderful parallel
of the state of the Reformation controversy, and that we
are on the Anti-Catholic side." [11] And in the *The Development of Christian Doctrine,* he writes: "To be deep in
history is to cease being a Protestant." [12]

Also essential for his conversion were his thoughts on
the certitude of conviction, for which he cites three conditions:

Certitude of conviction follows examination and proof.

11. W. H. Van de Pol, *Die Kirche im Leben und Denken Newmans,*
Salzburg, 1937, p. 218.
12. *Development of Christian Doctrine,* London, 1878.

It is accompanied by a sense of intellectual satisfaction and quiet.

It is irrevocable and lasting.

The first two conditions were fulfilled by Newman. The third one prompted another conclusion in him: the necessity of intellectual intolerance against that which is opposed to the truth of which one is certain.

Lastly, however, what decided Newman's conversion was not a set of subjective convictions, but the reality of the Church:

> This is the great, manifest, historical phenomenon which converted me,—to which all particular inquiries converged. Christianity is not a matter of opinion, but an external fact, entering into, carried out in, indivisible from, the history of the world. It has a bodily occupation of the world; it is one continuous fact or thing, the same from first to last, distinct from everything else: to be a Christian is to partake of, to submit to, this thing; and the simple question was, Where, what is this thing in this age, which in the first age was the Catholic Church?[13]

The question now arises: In what manner did Newman the Catholic take up his position opposite the Anglican Church? The ecumenical importance of Newman stands out clearly on this point. His conversion did not make him aware of any change in himself in either intellectual or moral matters. The acceptance of the Catholic faith was for him not a rejection of any truth in the faith of his

---

13. *Difficulties of Anglicans*, Vol. I, London, 1879, p. 368.

forefathers, no renunciation of anything positive which up to then he had loved and revered, no radical break with those he left behind in the Church of England. In his opinion, the Anglican Church was related to the Catholic Church as prophecy is related to fulfillment. His conversion did not mean to him the acceptance of a new faith but a true deliverance, a widening out and fulfillment in the one Church of God in which all truth, all goodness and beauty in the world has its place and its value.

Newman is convinced that even men outside the Church possess some partial truth which they hold as their own certitude. Catholic truth in its fullness and purity exists only in the Church, but even in denominations other than the Roman Catholic faith there can be found fragments of the one true Church (*vestigia ecclesiae*).

Reading in the writings of the Catholic Newman, one can see that he took seriously the problems of people who belonged to other denominations and that he was convinced this was not inconsistent with his principle of the intolerance of certitude toward untruth. A similar conviction motivated his attempt to understand the partner in a dialogue. Newman believed that even people who stand outside the Church can be recipients of extraordinary graces. There are saintly people outside the Church, and therefore Newman believed that a person who is convinced he is in the true Church which alone can assure salvation, will attain salvation from God even though the decision of his conscience is in error.

In this, Newman stood on the firm ground of ancient Catholic tradition. It must be added, however, that this thinking did not prevent Newman from attempting to lead other people to the Catholic Church. After all, the essence

of Christianity is the telling of its truth. During his Catholic years, Newman did not at first expect unification to be
in the form of a corporate return of the Anglican Church
to the Catholic Church. Having passed through the school
of great disappointments, he considered for the moment
individual conversion as the more likely possibility for
men to arrive at the totality of revealed truth. Nevertheless, Newman's goal was not the greatest possible harvest
of converts. In his letters he cited a number of reasons for
this attitude. In 1857 he writes to a friend:

> I think it is for the *interest* of Catholicism
> that individuals should not join us, but should
> remain to leaven the mass. I mean that they
> will do more for us by remaining where they
> are.[14]

Seen from this viewpoint and with this great goal in
mind, it might indeed be better that certain persons do
not become Catholics. On the other side there is, of course,
the particular salvation of each individual soul. And so he
writes:

> But then they have individual souls, and with
> what heart can I do anything to induce them
> to preach to others, if they themselves there-
> by become castaways?[15]

From these passages it is clear that this whole question
cannot be solved for Newman with a simple either-or.
"It could never be," he said shortly before his conversion,

>   that so large a portion of Christendom should

---

14. E. S. Purcell, *Life and Letters of Ambrose Phillips de Lisle*, Vol. I,
London, 1900, p. 368.
15. *Ibid.*

> have split off from the communion of Rome,
> and kept up a protest for 300 years for noth-
> ing . . . All aberrations are founded on, and
> have their life in, some truth or other—and
> Protestantism, so widely spread and so long
> enduring, must have in it, and must be witness
> for, a great truth or much truth.[16]

To make his views on this question better understood,
Newman wrote in 1863:

> My objects, my theory of acting, my powers,
> go in a different direction, and not one under-
> stood or contemplated at Rome. . . . To me,
> conversions are not the first thing, but the
> edification of Catholics. So much have I fixed
> upon the latter as my object, that up to this
> time the world persists in saying that I rec-
> ommend Protestants not to become Catholics.
> And, when I have given as my true opinion,
> that I am afraid to make hasty converts of
> educated men, lest they should not have
> counted the cost, and should have difficulties
> after they have entered the Church, I do but
> imply the same thing, that the Church must
> be prepared for converts, as well as converts
> prepared for the Church.[17]

This thought dominated all the ecumenical efforts of
Newman the Catholic. He was convinced that the Church
would gain new members only by way of personal pastoral

---

16. *Apologia*, p. 188.
17. Wilfrid Ward, *The Life of J. H. Newman*, London, 1913, Vol. 1,
p. 584.

care, and only when it prepared itself to receive converts. He was of the opinion that the Church—or better expressed, the Catholics—were not yet ready for the return of the separated Churches; maybe only catastrophes would bring about this readiness. For this reason, he considered his special duty within the Catholic sphere to be the education of Catholics as well as the overcoming of their narrow denominational outlook with its negative attitude toward other confessions. Newman's goal was to lead his fellow Catholics to a higher form of faith and love and knowledge. His aim was the purified Church of the future.

The Problem of an Ecumenical Theology

In 1847, Newman, who had in the meantime studied Catholic theology in Rome and had been ordained a priest, wrote to a professor of dogmatics in Rome that he was fully aware that he was not a theologian even though he was attempting, as much as was in his power, to treat theological problems in his books precisely and with care. He wanted to say that he was not a dogmatist bound to any particular system, nor a moral theologian in the strict sense of the word, nor a professor of theology. Since Newman was not attached to any particular system, he had to maintain a judicious position toward every theological system.

What Newman actually criticizes about the "systems" is their imprisonment in mere conceptions. A systematized treatment of the doctrine of faith can fall all too easily into the danger of considering things only as they currently are. Newman, however, attempted to illuminate being itself. The object of his thinking always was concrete man and the living God as He confronts us. For Newman, therefore, there is nothing that is finished, closed, complete; he continually meets new problems.

In his works, Newman distinguished between "real" and "abstract" and tried to shed light on inner relationships and order. The relation between religion and theology, piety and intellectual culture, living faith and scientific commitment—these were the urgent and painful concerns which motivated Newman, particularly during his Catholic years. They also were the motives that inspired all his works during this period, says Heinrich Fries. Newman's interests are centered not primarily on the various ideas themselves, but on the realization of these ideas in life and in history.

One of the most essential concepts in Newman's theology is the word "realization." Realization means for him bringing to life the supernatural within ourselves in the realities that confront us. What matters for each person is to make this reality his own. There is for Newman, therefore, no such thing as a mere conceptual, mere theoretical behavior, no mere superficial, noncomittal contact between the ego and the world, the "I" and God. Never is it permitted in matters of religion to behave abstractly or theoretically. With this concept Newman stands directly in the line of Augustine, Anselm, Bonaventure, and Martin Luther, as far as his fundamental principles are concerned.

In matters of religion, a mere conceptual, theoretical attitude is unacceptable. Newman's theological thinking is directed not toward the abstract, but toward the personal level. He did not lose himself in mere ideas and abstractions; he did not, for instance, construct any proofs for the existence of God, but he occupied himself constantly with the history of salvation which came to us through the incarnation and the life, death, and resurrection of Christ. His theological thinking is oriented toward the history of salvation.

Herein lies Newman's great importance for ecumenical activity. Whenever Catholic theology wants to express the truth of Revelation in a language that can be understood by the separated Christians, it will have to attempt to present the deposit of the faith in such a way that it brings the history of salvation into contact with the individual person, as Holy Scripture suggests. Newman did just that, and he is therefore the ideal interpreter between the various confessions.

Consider, for example, his concept of dogma: Dogma is for Newman the revealed reality of Christ. A life that is rooted in Revelation produces growth. Since the ascension of Christ into heaven, new questions have been posed and new answers have been given. Nevertheless, the fullness of faith was already present in the spirit of the Apostles, indeed throughout all times, but more as a matter of feeling and unconscious intuition, that is to say implicitly and not in the form of precise formulations and as an intellectually tangible whole. Only when a concrete question arose, did the Apostles and their successors find themselves forced to examine what their thinking up to then had been.

Dogmas, therefore, are never abstract theses hanging loosely and disconnectedly in the air. Every dogma is based on a divine reality, expresses a fact established by Christ for all times. But this fact can never be perfectly or completely expressed by a dogma. Even countless dogmas could neither fathom nor exhaust even one fact of salvation, for instance the fact that Christ is the Son of God.

In this Church here on earth, immediate contemplation of God is not yet our lot. But because every dogma is based on a divine reality, man cannot accept one dogma and reject another. The rejection of a single dogmatic truth would imply that the other truths are being only apparently accepted; it would mean that there is no reality underlying the profession of any dogma. Dogmas are not intellectual conclusions; they are an expression of the fact that certain truths, which heretofore were believed unconsciously and implicitly, have now been consciously accepted and even formulated. It is therefore impossible to find a scriptural text for each and every dogmatic statement. Holy Scripture begins a series of developments but never completes any of them.

What becomes visible in Newman's theological thought is this: Formulations are not ends in themselves. The formulation of dogmatic sentences is for him like teaching with stammering lips, as he says in the *Via media*, because he was filled in all his depths with the reality of faith which transcends all formulation. The mysterium cannot be exhausted by men. What moved Newman to believe in the Divine reality that confronts us in Revelation and in the sacraments was not some formulated dogma, rather the reverse is true: From the reality of the Revelation he arrives at faith, and through faith he can accept the formulated dogmas of the Church. More sublime than all formulated dogma is the mystical sacramental reality. But with this position, Newman in no way deprecates the dogmas and doctrinal theses of the Church. "Purity of faith is more precious to the Christian even than unity," he writes in his *Apologia*. But for Newman the invisible is so real that it has precedence over the visible.

In this light it may perhaps also be possible to understand Newman's difficulties with Cardinal Manning. In 1851 Manning became a Catholic—six years after Newman; he studied in Rome and in 1865 was named Archbishop of Westminster and made a cardinal, as successor to Wiseman. The Roman Catholic Church was faced with great difficulties during the years of its revival in England. The burning problem for both Cardinal Wiseman and Cardinal Manning was this: How can the unity in the life of the Church be preserved and strengthened? This meant that the external unity of the Church had to be emphasized. For that reason they aimed at firmly anchoring the external guarantees: the visible unity of the Church in liturgy, doctrine, preaching, and theology. Newman also was convinced of the necessity of these external testimonies, but he felt himself much less bound to them than did Catholics of Manning's type. Newman lived by the immediate, unalterable, and undivided divine reality which permeates and upholds the visible Church, its offices and its sacraments.

It has been said that the principle of analogy was the foundation of Newman's thinking. By analogy Newman means the relationship between natural religion and revealed religion. This reciprocity finds the ultimate source of its unity in God, who is the God both of creation and redemption, and in man, who belongs to both worlds. Therefore, Newman's thought embraces both these spheres, that of grace and of nature, of revelation and of the concrete man. Heinrich Fries comments on this point in his essay,

"Newman's Theological Significance": "How fruitful and redeeming a theology would be which, in the spirit of Newman, would attempt, perhaps even accomplish, something similar today: a theology which would translate the analogy of nature and grace into the existential language of our time, a theology which would be sensitive to the hidden needs of Christian and human existence, and would open the way to the Christian faith for the man of today who is foundering or has foundered on the meaning of his existence." [18] Nature and grace are not seen by Newman as two layers, one on top of the other, as though nature were something like a lower floor and grace the higher floor that belongs to it. Important for an ecumenical theology, however, is its transmission onto the existential level. Wherever this concern comes clearly through in Catholic theology, there is a bridge capable of carrying the weight of our mutual thoughts: a bridge to the thinking of our Protestant brethren for whom it is so important that they see creation and redemption, God the creator and God the redeemer, in their oneness.

The Problem of the Catholicity of the Church

What the ecumenical movement needs for success has been summed up by one German Protestant and theologian as follows: "When in both its faith and life the Roman Church is truly catholic, not narrowly Catholic and anti-Protestant, when the Churches of the Reformation are truly Evangelical, not only protesting and anti-Roman, and when the Churches of the East are truly

18. *Ibid.*, p. 186.

apostolic, not just rigidly Orthodox or Eastern—then the foundation stone of unity will have indeed been laid." What matters to Catholics, therefore, is that they become ever more reflectively aware of the fullness of their own faith, that they become truly and fully Catholic, that is to say, all-embracing in both the vertical and horizontal meaning of the word: reaching down, reaching up, reaching out. Cardinal Newman is *the* prototype of this truly Catholic man. In his own life he exemplified some of the genuine concerns of the Reformation: the meaning of conscience, the personal experience of the I-Thou relationship between man and God, and the immediate experience of the sacred as it communicates itself to man. Newman realizes these very real concerns of the Reformation in a Catholic way; that is to say, in their fullness.

The role and importance of *conscience* stand at the center of Newman's thought. By conscience he means the immediacy of God's call to man, and the personal experience of divine authority. Often quoted is his statement in a letter to the Duke of Norfolk: "If I am obliged to bring religion into after-dinner toasts. . . . I shall drink—to the Pope, if you please,—still to conscience first, and to the Pope afterwards." [19] Nonetheless, as much as Newman emphasizes the importance of conscience, nothing is further from his mind than to see in conscience an autonomous, uncommitted judge. Newman holds that in meeting his conscience man experiences God the judge and redeemer, that is, the law-giving voice of God. This experience requires from conscience an unconditional listening to the God who commands.

But who transmits the will of God to man? The voice

---

19. Open Letter to Duke of Norfolk, Freiburg 1875, p. 3.

of conscience was obscured by the original sin of the first man, and it is therefore unsure. Our conscience, it follows, is fallible. Newman experiences God's demand, and God's authority, in the Church. On this point he differs with Sören Kierkegaard, who took his position just as passionately against the Church as Newman did in favor of the Church and its role as helper to the individual in his encounter with God.

Insofar as he sees conscience bound to the word of God in the Old and New Testament, Newman is in agreement with Luther. But, to speak in Newman's terms, the word of God reaches man through the Holy Spirit in Christ and reveals itself in the Church. Because Newman bases the Church on the incarnation of Christ, Christ for him is still tangible in the Church today, through the Holy Spirit. This distinguishes Newman's thought from any Protestant concept which holds that God reveals Himself directly to each man. "Protestants maintain," he writes, "that Our Lord Himself is all in all, evidence and proof, as well as Object, of our faith. . . ." Far from putting aside such an "experimental knowledge of Christ," he continues, "I should myself consider that this personal hold upon Him is the immediate evidence of Divine truth to every true consistent Christian, who has no need of having his answer in hand to every one of the multiform objections which from day to day he may hear urged against his faith."

(But Newman is too much a man of sober realism not to know that this ideal state of union with Christ does not exist permanently in history. So he goes on to say):

But I consider too that the Lover of Souls and

Searcher of Hearts has not thought it enough for us, has not felt it safe for our poor nature, to have no other safeguard for our faith than this. Religious experiences and convictions, when right, come from God—but Satan can counterfeit them . . . and, in matter of fact, men who have professed the most beautiful things and with the utmost earnestness and sincerity believed in their union with Our Lord, have often slipped away into one or other form of error on the grounds of their new inward experiences and convictions—not only into one or other form of misbelief, but into scepticism and infidelity. . . . Here it is that I see the wisdom and mercy of God in setting up a Catholic Church for the protection of his elect children. . . .[20]

Because of the experience of the divine will acting in the individual conscience occurs in a rather vague, shadowy way, conscience finds its fulfillment only in its subjection to a visible divine authority: the authority of the visible Church.

Thus we find the Catholic synthesis realized in Newman: conscience *and* external authority, and this synthesis leads directly to another synthesis: that between interior and exterior life. Protestantism tends to downgrade the external, the visible—whatever is apparent—in favor of the interior, the invisible. In one of his sermons, Newman poses the question whether the ministry, the imitation (of Christ), the sacrament, the rite and the ceremonial are

---

20. Ward, *The Life of J. H. Newman,* Vol. II, pp. 393–394.

not perhaps external forms only, and he answers:

> We call it a form only so long as we refuse to
> walk by *faith,* which dispenses with things
> visible. Faith sees things not to be forms, if
> commanded, which seem like forms; it real-
> izes consequences.[21]

Therein precisely lies the real reason for the disunity
of the Church—not that the individual's faith is too little,
but that everything which in reality is a great mystery of
imperishable value, is looked upon as mere exterior form.

> But now multitudes, both in and without the
> Church, have set it up on high as a great dis-
> covery, and glory in it as a great principle,
> that forms are worth nothing. They allow
> themselves to wander about from one com-
> munion to another, or from church to meet-
> ing-house, and make it a boast that they
> belong to no party and are above all parties.[22]

Through his studies of the Fathers of the Church Newman had arrived at the realization that the Church is a
spiritual, invisible world made constantly alive and visible
in time. The visible and the invisible are most intimately
joined in the Church.

Newman also was Catholic, all-embracing, in relation
to the *past,* the history of the Church. He recognized the
fullness of the Church's life in the entirety of its history.
No longer—as during his Anglican years—did a certain
period of the Church, the first centuries, for example,

---

21. *Parochial and Plain Sermons,* Vol. III, p. 195.
22. *Ibid.,* Vol. 7, p. 241.

constitute for him the decisive and original historical reality. But because he now accepted the entire history of the Church, he also had to find a positive attitude toward his own past. His conversion to Catholicism, therefore, did not result in an absolute break with those he left behind in the Anglican Church.

> All this is quite consistent with believing, as firmly as I do, that individuals in the English Church are invisibly knit into that True Body of which they are not outwardly members.[23]

> What can I say but that those great and burning truths which I learned when a boy from Evangelical teaching, I have found impressed upon my heart with fresh and ever increasing force by the Holy Roman Church? That Church has added to the simple Evangelicalism of my first teachers, but it has obscured, diluted, enfeebled, nothing of it.[24]

But Newman is Catholic in relation to the *future* as well. He stands openly for all that means progress and development. It was this characteristic which made his position in the English Catholicism of the time rather difficult. He became a symbol in the struggle between the progressive and the reactionary forces. His biographer, Ward, quotes him as once saying:

> We are in a strange time. I have not a shadow of misgiving that the Catholic Church and its doctrine are directly from God—but then I

23. *Letters*, Vol. II, p. 419.
24. *Ward*, Vol. II, p. 527.

know well that there is in particular quarters
a narrowness which is not of God. And I believe great changes before now have taken
place in the direction of the Church's course,
and that new aspects of her aboriginal doctrines have suddenly come forth, and all this
co-incidentally with changes in the world's
history, such as are now in progress; so that
I never should shut up, when new views are
set before me, though I might not take them
as a whole.[25]

Because of this stand, Newman's life as a Catholic was
a life of great suffering. He was under suspicion from all
sides of not being strictly Catholic. He was accused of
preaching a secularized Catholicism, and reactionary circles considered him *the* danger in English Catholicism.

The catholicity in his attitude became evident also
when he demanded for England a Catholicism that would
take into account the individuality of the English. He
saw danger in the attitude of bishops who considered it
their duty to impose on their flocks not only that which
pertained to faith and morals, but also Roman devotional
practices. His opposition against such influences was
sharp. Through close contacts with ecclesiastical representatives from the Northern countries, he aimed to
achieve a counterweight to Catholicism as it was then
practiced in Rome and in the Southern countries.

With apprehension therefore, he followed the efforts
in behalf of the proclamation of the dogma of papal infallibility. In a confidential letter to Bishop Ullathorne,

---

25. *Ibid.* Vol. I, p. 439.

Newman expressed what worried him during the Vatican Council:

> Rome ought to be a name to lighten the heart at all times, and a Council's proper office is, when some great heresy or other evil impends, to inspire the faithful with hope and confidence. But now we have the greatest meeting which has ever been, and that in Rome, infusing into us by the accredited organs of Rome (such as the *Civilta,* the *Armonia,* the *Universe,* and the *Tablet*) little else than fear and dismay. Where we are all at rest and have no doubts, and, at least practically, not to say doctrinally, hold the Holy Father to be infallible, suddenly there is thunder in the clear sky, and we are told to prepare for something, we know not what, to try our faith, we know not how. No impending danger is to be averted, but a great difficulty is to be created. Is this the proper work for an Ecumenical Council? As to myself personally, please God, I do not expect any trial at all, but I cannot help suffering with the various souls that are suffering. . . . When has definition of doctrine *de fide* been a luxury of devotion and not a stern, painful necessity. Why should an aggressive and insolent faction be allowed to make the hearts of the just to mourn whom the Lord hath not made sorrowful? Why can't we be let alone when we have pursued peace and thought no evil? I assure you, my dear Lord, some of the tru-

> est minds are driven one way and another,
> and do not know where to rest their feet.[26]

Here Newman speaks in the first place as one entrusted with the care for souls. He looked at a Roman pronouncement not as something abstract but as something related to the spiritual welfare of the faithful. Many people, foremost among them the professor of theology, Döllinger in Munich, but also some of his Anglican friends were confronted with great difficulties because of the new dogma. The Anglicans believed that all thoughts of reunion had now to be abandoned. Newman's misgivings were centered mostly on pastoral considerations. Like St. Paul who, even though directly inspired, was worried lest his words might harm his new converts in Corinth, so he too feared very much now, he wrote, that the infallible voice of the Council might do harm to the cause of the Church in Germany, England, and other places.

The dogma as such caused Newman's faith not the least difficulties, but he considered its pronouncement inopportune. Because of this candor, he was for years looked upon with disfavor in the Catholic Church. His plans for the education of Catholics, as, for example, the plans for a Catholic university in Dublin or for a Catholic college at Oxford, met time and again with failure, due not least to suspicions brought against him in Rome. In letters to friends which Newman wrote at that time, we find these reflections:

> . . . It is still the blessed will of God to send me baulks. On the whole, I suppose, looking through my life as a course, he is using me,

---

26. *Ibid.* Vol. II, pp. 287–288.

but really viewed in its separate parts it is but a life of failures. . . .

And to another friend:

It is sad to hear anyone speak as if his work was done, and he was but waiting to go . . . , for what does one live for except to work? . . . What influence should I have with Protestants and Infidels, if a pack of Catholic critics opened at my back fiercely, saying that this remark was illogical, that unheard of, a third realistic, a fourth idealistic, a fifth sceptical, and a sixth temerarious, or shocking to pious ears?[27]

Thus it came about that in 1862 a rumor appeared in the press: Newman intended to return to the Anglican Church because he was not understood in the Catholic Church. In answer to these rumors, Newman published the following statement:

I have not had one moment's wavering of trust in the Catholic Church ever since I was received into her fold. I hold, and ever have held, that the Sovereign Pontiff is the centre of unity and the Vicar of Christ; and I have ever had, and have still, an unclouded faith in her creed in all its articles; a supreme satisfaction in her worship, discipline, and teaching; and an eager longing, a hope against hope, that the many dear friends whom I left in Protestantism may be partakers of my happiness.[28]

27. *Ibid.* Vol. II, pp. 67, 254.
28. *Ibid.* Vol. I, p. 580.

But now a great accusation, namely that of hypocrisy, was flung against Newman by an Anglican, and it brought a sudden turn in his life. In 1864, within a few weeks of concentrated labor, from the middle of April to the beginning of June, often of sixteen or more hours a day, Newman wrote his defense: the *Apologia Pro Vita Sua.* It was of such compelling candor that, all at once, it won him the hearts of his countrymen. In the *Apologia* Newman not only intended to refute the accusation against himself, but he also set out to eliminate the prejudices against the Catholic Church in general, while simultaneously presenting a history of his religious convictions. All this his book accomplished perfectly. No work has so restored the position of the Catholics in England's intellectual life and so raised respect for them as the *Apologia.* Now Newman was praised on all sides as the defender of the faith. Yet in 1868, it was rumored again that Newman would remain no longer in the Roman Church. At that time he answered:

> I have found in the Catholic Church abundance of courtesy, but very little sympathy, among persons in high place, except a few— but there is a depth and a power in the Catholic religion, a fulness of satisfaction in its creed, its theology, its rites, its sacraments, its discipline, a freedom yet a support also, before which the neglect or the misapprehension about oneself on the part of individual living persons, however exalted, is as so much dust, when weighed in the balance. This is the true secret of the Church's strength, the

principle of its indefectibility, and the bond
of its indissoluble unity. It is the earnest and
the beginning of the repose of heaven.[29]

Through many years Newman endured misunderstanding and lack of appreciation without wavering even for
a moment in his mission or in his faith. And in spite of
all his difficulties he did not become bitter. The source
of this humility and this unshakable piety was the same
that caused him all the misunderstanding in the first place:
namely his unquestioning, unqualified faith in the hidden
reality of the Church. This faith dominated his life.
Therein lies his greatness as a man and as a Christian.
The rejections he suffered forced him back again and
again to the inner reality of all things, and through this
process he reached the heights.

Then a change occurred on the papal throne, and it
was to be of great significance for Newman. The suggestion to make him a cardinal was put forward and it found
immediate appeal. In 1879, Pope Leo XIII acceded to the
universal request. Through Cardinal Nina, the pontiff
wrote to Newman:

Most Reverend Father: In deep appreciation
of your intellect and your scholarly work,
your piety and your zeal in the service of
God, your devotion and loyalty to the Holy
Apostolic See and the eminent services you
have rendered through so many years to our
Holy religion, the Holy See has resolved to
confer on you a public and solemn proof of

29. *Ibid.* Vol. II, p. 201.

> its esteem and benevolence. To this end the Holy See is pleased to elevate you to the honors of the Sacred Purple.
>
> While imparting this message to you, I congratulate you . . . and shall be delighted to see you soon in the Senate of the Holy Church as one of its main luminaries.

From all that has here been recalled, it is obvious how much Newman can help us to clarify the working methods and the goal of ecumenical activity on the Catholic side. This is possible chiefly because Newman's entire theological thinking reflects the reality he experienced and lived. Thought and realization are indivisible in Newman. What ought to be of utmost importance for Catholics, however, is not in the first place Newman's conversion to the Catholic Church, but his whole attitude toward the separated brethren. Newman took all the positive values from his ancestral Anglican Church with him and remained wholly himself. Thus he was able to unfold within the Catholic community the ecumenical breadth of true catholicity. And Newman could do these things because he never lived in extremes. His personal character as well as his scholarly thinking were centered on a "middle ground," the *via media*—not in the sense of hazy compromises, but rather in an attitude of constant striving to do justice to all sides of a phenomenon and to all the facts of a case, in order to see the whole picture, and thereby the truth. Thus it was possible that, with only minor exceptions, even his Anglican works could be added without changes to the treasury of Catholic literature.

Even more humanly engaging and compelling is the

openness in Newman's character. In human relations, truthfulness is the bridge from man to man. The airing of contrary opinions is not at all incompatible with this principle, for it is a consequence of inner truthfulness that differing opinions can be treated with respect and with charity.

The secret of Newman's impact lies in the unique combination of genius and holiness, of total humanity and total Christianity, both harmoniously joined.

Strolling through the cloister of the Oratory in Birmingham (which Newman joined as a Catholic), and reading the memorial tablets there, one can find among them also the one in memory of Newman with the inscription he himself had chosen: "Ex umbris et imaginibus in veritatem"—"from shadows and images to the truth." And on his simple grave stone is engraved his motto: "Cor ad cor loquitur"—"heart speaks to heart." Looking back on the life of this man, no one can be tempted to read any kind of sentimentality into these words; sentimentality was not his nature. He simply meant by these words the bridge the human heart must build to human heart, from man to man. It is Newman's way of expressing the relationship wherein the heart, as the center of man, is joined to the heart of God and to that of his fellow man. In this way—so we hope—can Church and Church also become "one heart and one soul."

6

THOMAS
SARTORY, OSB

TOWARD
UNITY
IN FAITH

THERE RUNS THROUGH the Church today, like a new pentecostal awakening, the desire to overcome its disunity in
faith. Pentecostal awakening—this makes us think of what
Holy Scripture says of the Holy Spirit, who on the world's
first Pentecost day came down on the fledgling Church
to gather what was scattered, to impart the word which
put an end to the confusion of tongues.

In the chapel of the Ecumenical Institute in Heidelberg,
Germany, are two stained-glass windows. Over the altar,
on the wall behind it, is a presentation of the descent of
the Holy Spirit on the Apostles on Pentecost day. As the
faithful stand with their faces towards the altar, which is
the symbol of Christ manifested in word and sacrament,
they behold the pentecostal in-gathering of those that
were dispersed. But when they turn their backs to the
altar they see, set into the back wall of the chapel, a picture of the Babylonian dispersion.

Is this not a telling symbol of what is happening in our
own day? Christians of all Churches and denominations
are looking for ways to overcome their division. They see
the spectacle of Babel in a new clarity today. They know
that human ability and intellectual power do not conquer

heaven. So they turn to Christ, the Lord and Savior and Redeemer; they pray for the coming of the kingdom of God in this world and in this time. Anew they hear the saving message of the Gospel: that the Good Shepherd "in his arms shall gather the lambs" (Is. 40: 11). And because they know that only God can heal their disunity, Christians are uniting in prayer to implore the Spirit of God. Every year in January they all—Catholics, Orthodox, Anglicans, and Protestants—observe the World Unity Octave. But their unanimous prayer for unity is not all; Christians are also searching for ways to bridge the cleavages between them.

In what follows we shall see the story of two great endeavors—one Evangelical and Protestant, the other Catholic—toward unity.

The Protestant world has signified its desire for unity through the ecumenical movement and the World Council of Churches. Some 170 Protestant denominations and several Orthodox Churches are cooperating in this search for unity on the common basis of faith in Jesus Christ, their God and Savior. At a meeting in Toronto in July, 1950, the Central Committee of the World Council of Churches accepted an exposition on the meaning of the Council for the participating Churches. The Ecumenical Council of the World Council of Churches is an attempt, so states this declaration, to approach the problem of inter-Church relations in a new way without precedent in history. That explains why its intent and its character can easily be misunderstood. It would be difficult to arrive at a precise explanation of why the Churches have refrained from defining the nature of the Church exactly and in detail. The difficulty was how to determine the ecclesiastical significance of a corporate body in which considerably varying concepts of the nature of the Church are represented, without making use of the specific formulas of one or the other of these concepts.

The document begins by saying what the World Council is *not:* The Council is neither a super-Church nor a worldwide Church, nor is it the One Holy Church of which the Creed speaks. As proof of this it is stated: "The Council does not possess any ecclesiastical judicial powers and is not authorized to act in the name of the Churches. It is not a body that can make decisions." Its task is rather to bring the Churches into contact with each other and to draw them into discussion on questions of Christian unity. There is room, therefore, within the Ecumenical Council of Churches for the concept of a Church which represents every "member church"; its basis is simply the belief in our Lord Jesus Christ as God and Savior. This foundation must be accepted by all member Churches. Membership in the Council, therefore, does not negate the individual Church's concept of itself. The problem of truth is in no way ruled out, and it would be a misunderstanding to assume that the ecumenical movement would advocate doctrinal or conceptual uniformity of all Christian Churches. When a Church becomes a member of the Council, this does not mean that it has to accept a certain doctrinal definition in regard to the nature of Church unity. The Council allows for the most varied concepts of Church unity.

On the positive side this much is stated:

Christ is the Divine head of His body, the Church. Relations between the Churches cannot have stability and promise unless they begin by jointly acknowledging in humility that Christ is the head of His Church. Since the member Churches believe on the word of the New Testament that the Church of Jesus Christ is one, it simply is the Christian duty of every Church to do its utmost to make this unity of the Church visible. For this reason, the task of the ecumenical movement consists in seeking union with all those who belong together as members of the same Mystical Body, even though they are not members of the same visible body. The ecumenical movement is the place where this search and this discovery occur.

From this membership in the World Council of Churches it does not follow, however, that every member Church has to recognize each of the other member Churches as "Church" in the full meaning of the word. Within the Council there is room for such recognition as well as for withholding it. The member Churches of the Council are willing to work for a common witness to their common Lord. And from their common membership flows the practical conclusion that the members know themselves united by a bond of solidarity, will come to each other's aid when this is needed, and will refrain from acts which would be harmful to their fraternal relations. Thus, the member Churches are brought into a spiritual relationship wherein they endeavor to learn from each other and to help one another.

For the Protestant confessions, which cover a tremendous range in both doctrine and ecclesiastical constitutions—from the Lutherans to the Quakers—the Toronto document is a good basis on which to proceed with the search for Church unity. The Catholic Church is not a participant in the World Council of Churches. This aloofness, however, should not be misunderstood as a haughty or belittling attitude; its motives are exclusively of a dogmatic nature. That is to say, the Catholic Church believes that it is itself the realization of the Church of Jesus Christ in history and that therefore the unity of the Church is not something that has to be sought, as though it did not already exist. However, the Catholic Church follows with keen interest the developments within the Protestant ecumenical movement.[1]

There are also points where the intentions of the World Council of Churches converge with those of Rome. Pope Pius XII's discourses on the subject of a just peace, the use of atomic and nuclear weapons, and on the spirit of technology coincide with corresponding utterances in documents of the World Council, sometimes almost verbatim.

As already stated, the Catholic Church has a clearly defined doctrine in regard to the unity of the Church. The question, therefore, is whether it is at all possible to enter into a dialogue with the Catholic Church, for its concept of unity requires it to call the separated brethren back to the paternal home: its own fold.

At this point, a brief word is in order regarding the Catholic Una Sancta movement because in it is exemplified the Catholic position in the work for unity, and because it is, in the words of the Lutheran professor of theology, Ernst Kinder, "a necessary supplementation of the ecumenical movement, as long as the Catholic Church cannot participate in the latter." For, says Kinder, "we simply

---

1. In recent years the Catholic Church has sent official observers to the major meetings of the World Council which, in turn, is sending its official observers to all the sessions of the Second Vatican Council. (Publisher's note.)

need the contact and the discussions with the Roman Catholic Church because in some decisive points it has better safeguarded and preserved the Christian substance."

The Una Sancta movement furthers the meeting of Christians of various confessions, but at the same time it aims at more than mere meeting. It is this "more," both hoped for and aimed at, which makes the Una Sancta movement what it is, and distinguishes it from other encounters between adherents of the various Christian denominations, in say, the cultural or political spheres.

Una Sancta—this means the One, Holy, Catholic, and Apostolic Church which we profess in the Creed. In spite of all differences in the concrete understanding of this one Church, on one point all Christians within this movement are united: Christ has founded only one Church. Because there is only one head, Christ, there can therefore be only one Church which belongs to Him as His body. There is unanimity between the Protestant and Catholic members of the movement on the understanding that the Church unity which would correspond to the intent of Christ, its founder, cannot be restricted to the realm of the invisible, but must also be a visible reality.

But the opinions of the Catholic and Protestant members of the movement divide over such questions as: Which is this one Church? Where is it? Or: How can this one Church be reconstituted? The name of the movement stands for a program, but on the question as to how this is to be understood, no unity is in sight. For the Catholic this program can, in the last analysis, only mean the reunion of all Christians in the bosom of that Holy, Catholic, and Apostolic Church which Christ Himself founded on the rock of Peter. For the Protestant Christian, on the other hand, this is precisely the concept he cannot accept; he is convinced that the Church of the popes is not the legitimate place of reunion.

It is remarkable that a movement in which such contrary tendencies are present has not been dissolved long ago by its own contradictions. But one unifying ferment is clearly at work in it: "God wills it." Because the division and dissension of Christians is clearly "the thing that must not be." The spark, once ignited, cannot die. Christians want to unite with Christians because this is Christ's will. Something has come to life. Something has been set in motion. It is not just a club that has been founded or any other kind of organization. There are no by-laws in the Una Sancta movement, no membership cards or dues— only men and women in whom something has been awakened that will never again come to rest.

If we as believing Christians, whether Catholic or Protestant, speak of reunion in faith, we mean a real growing together into one body, not merely a superficial getting together or fraternization under the motto: Let us forget what separates us; we all are, after all, children of God." No. But since we know that only God can effect union, it is understandable that the Una Sancta movement is, first of all, a movement of prayer and penance. The power of God knows no limitations, and to trusting prayer has been given the promise that it will move the mercy of God. Because it is a movement of prayer, there is none that would be unfit to be a member, if only he has the desire, the longing for the union of all Christians. The Una Sancta movement, however, is not only a place where Christians are called to prayers, it is also a movement where thought is given to how gulfs may be bridged. Una

Sancta brings Christians together for dialogue.

The task of our day is the *preparation* of union so that we, as far as it lies in us and as best we can, may remove the obstacles which block the way to future reunion. Perhaps it was necessary for us to learn before all else to look upon one another as brothers, to accept one another as brothers, to love one another as brothers.

Summing up, we may perhaps express it this way: The Una Sancta movement would like to see the Catholic become a better Catholic, to love his Church fully and utterly and to take root in it, and the Evangelical Christian to become more Protestant, to live out of the fullness of the Gospel without exhausting his energies in a rigid anti-Catholic stand. What God then will make of these Catholics and these Evangelical Christians, how and when He will lead them to visible unity in the one Church—that we can confidently leave to Him. The ecumenical movement and the Una Sancta both say: "To hope against hope, this is what our faith teaches us."

Doctrine

What most divides Christianity are different doctrines which are opposed to each other. Even if Christians can pray the Creed together, they must part ways when it comes to what they believe of the Church; they understand this doctrine in mutually exclusive ways. Many people in our time are puzzled by this. They look upon the doctrinal differences of the Christian denominations as useless theological squabbles, especially when they come to realize that these differences are often so subtle that a layman can hardly distinguish them. They are very aware of the fact that they live in the midst of a de-Christianized society, among men and women who have thrown all faith overboard and refuse to be led back to Christ by the abstract theses of academic teachers. To put it bluntly, unbelievers will not be convinced by what a Catholic bishop or a Protestant professor of theology *says*, but only by what he practices. The member of a sect standing Sunday after Sunday on a street corner trying to sell his tracts filled with a perhaps totally confused concept of Christian doctrine, or stumping from door to door to enlist interest for his sect, may impress a nonbeliever more than some Catholic who keeps boasting that his Church possesses all the truth, but who could not care less about that truth when it comes to being a witness to it in the concrete circumstances of everyday life.

This situation in which Christians often find themselves today, has to be kept in mind when we speak of doctrine and the importance of truth for the unity of the Church. The separated Christians are one in the conviction that there cannot and must not be any Church unity at the expense of truth. The Apostle Paul in his Epistle to the Ephesians describes the unity of the Church as given by *one* Lord, *one* faith, and *one* Baptism. Faith as a foundation for unity, in this context, is not the individual belief of an individual Christian, but is understood by the Apostle as an objectively established good, a rule, a doctrine "to which you have given yourselves," as it is phrased in the Epistle to the Romans. This doctrine is consolidated in the New Testament in formulated beliefs which will have to be accepted and preserved by the faithful. Yet, he who knows the doctrines of his Church or denomination well and even professes them, thus bearing witness to the truth, is not thereby already a Christian; for "truth" in the New Testament is more than right doctrine. It is well to keep this in mind while we pose the question of whether *unity in truth* is possible among Christians.

Truth, in the New Testament, is that which has stability and validity. Truth means certainty, constancy, sincerity, honesty. Whenever, therefore, Christians meet in sincerity and honesty, they meet in truth. In practice, this means that the separated Christians do not deal with each other as a matter of tactics or for reasons of ecclesiastical political considerations. On the other hand, it would be just as wrong to say "yes," where faith and conscience require us to say "no." Fuzzy indifferentism is counter to the truth. Constancy and sincerity are especially required in those situations where the Christian brother, regardless of the confession to which he belongs, is oppressed and persecuted by anti-Christian powers.

Truth, again according to the New Testament, is truthfulness in bearing witness. The opposite is a lie. Whenever a Christian, Catholic or Protestant, presents the factual teachings of his Church, there the separated Christians meet in truth. It follows that in the dialogue with the separated brethren the doctrine of the Church must be fully presented, substantiated, and explained, undiminished and without de-emphasizing anything for the sake of a superficial harmony. The Swiss Catholic Bishop Besson once admonished his Catholics:

> Let us not adulterate the teachings of the Church. One can find people among us who propagate certain religious practices border-

ing on superstition, certain extravagant prayer formulas, certain pseudo-prophecies which, incidentally, have never been approved by either the pope or the bishops. Such things make outsiders believe that our faith is a mixture of childishness and foolishness. Let us stand fast to the authentic doctrine of the Church; only in this way can we smooth the path to Christian unity for a good stretch of the road.

Much as a Christian is bound to the truth of his Church, his loyalty must avoid the pitfalls of fanaticism and sectarianism. It would, after all, be an arrogant and foolish presumption to assert that each individual Catholic is a true witness and infallible interpreter of the truth of the Church. Bishop Carriére said:

There are Catholics who, without being aware of it, assume for themselves the mantle of infallibility, so to speak, by claiming absolute validity for their personal interpretations of the Church's teachings. They go on making affirmations and denials as though the infallible Church was speaking through them— and in so doing they often disfigure, and almost always harden, the sublime and gentle face of truth.

And what is true of these statements concerning the truths of our own Church, applies equally to statements concerning the teachings and the religious forms of our separated brethren. We have the duty to declare error as error, but we should do so only after careful examination as to whether our separated brethren indeed teach and practice what we presume they teach and practice on any particular question.

In the Gospel and in the writings of John the Apostle, truth is above all equivalent to divine reality. In the eighth chapter of the Gospel of St. John it is said that truth gives life. And according to 1 John 1: 9, truth is a divine reality which does not dwell in liars. Here truth is, as it were, taken out of the context of mere knowable doctrine; it is completely personified, as Christ Himself said: "I *am* the way, and the truth, and the life" (John 14: 6), and is translated into ethics: "We *do* the truth" it is written by John in the third chapter of his Gospel and in his first Epistle; that is, we practice it. Truth is made evident to the world outside by moral corroboration.

Whenever the reality of God, the divine life, is infused into a Christian, whenever a man receives the grace of partaking in Jesus Christ, he stands in the realm of truth. This infusion of the divine life takes place in Baptism. And through Baptism, we all, whether Orthodox or Catholic or Lutheran or Anglican, are immersed in Jesus Christ. It can rightly be said, therefore, that Baptism is the great ecumenical sacrament. Thus, unity in faith grows whenever Christians grow more and more deeply into Jesus Christ who *is* the truth. And where the truth is "done," is lived, where genuine faith holds sway, there Catholics and non-Catholics stand already in the realm of truth.

But now let us consider what divides Christians.

Again according to the New Testament, truth also means right doctrine and right faith. Peter even speaks of obedience to truth. (1 Peter 1: 22).[2] Here begin the differences that divide us. But here also begins our task of examining exactly and carefully just what the doctrine of the other confession is. Protestant and Catholic theologians who for years have been carrying on dialogues among themselves, have already resolved many misunderstandings and prejudices. Catholics, too, can make a contribution here. They know that the doctrine of the Church, in so far as formulated theses are concerned, has often been drawn up in defense against some heresy. Thus, a number of decrees of the Council of Trent in the sixteenth century are directed against errors of the Reformation. The Council formulated its definitions in the most concise of forms and usually in a negative style: "He who says such and such is anathema." It is remarkable how sensitively the Council of Trent in its terse definitions weighed and took into account the legitimate concern for the revealed truth which, after all, is present in the nucleus of every heresy.

But the theologians and priests in the Church had to work with these definitions in the post-Tridentine age, and in this respect it cannot be overlooked that practical pastoral teaching and speculative theology did not always succeed in retaining the delicate balance of the conciliar decrees. It happened all too often that an extreme—and thereby wrong—assertion of the reformers was met with an equally extreme rebuttal. Heresy, which by nature is always onesided or extreme, thus presents to the Church an

2. Where the Douay translation renders this text: "Obedience to charity," the Jerusalem Bible, like the official German translations, renders it: "Purify your souls through *obedience to truth* in honest brotherly love." It is this latter translation on which the German author bases his thought. (Tr. note.)

all too easy and dangerous occasion for a similar onesided-
ness on its part. We Catholics must therefore realize that
even with us the use of a hardened or incomplete—that is,
partial—truth is possible in theology, in preaching, in the
practice of the faith. We, too, have the duty to proclaim
the superior totality of the truth in the face of all partial
truth and all error. This is an eminently ecumenical task.

The French Dominican, Congar, once described the nature of ecumenical work in this context by means of an
analogy. He applied what Gilson wrote about the contrast between Augustinism and Thomism, and said:

> The exponents of thoughts that contradict
> one another must be given the necessary time
> to understand each other better, indeed to
> understand themselves better, so that they
> may come to terms at a point which is not yet
> visible today, but which lies certainly in the
> path of their present line of thinking.

Congar is of the opinion that a Catholic theologian can
accept this formula. The dogmatic position of his Church
requires him to hold fast to the conviction that this point,
although not as yet visible in the historically unfolding
deposit of the faith, is nonetheless already present in his
Church, which is the Church of the Apostles. While it is
true, therefore, that some things will undergo a change,
it is not permissible to demand from anyone that he relinquish any of the doctrines which he has received from
his Church and which he holds true. To change—yet not
to change! "There is a solution to this antimony; its name
is development," an Anglican author wrote not long ago
speaking of the Catholic Church. It cannot change, he

wrote, but "it can explain itself better. It is my firm conviction that many things which at the present time contribute to our division, can be clarified in such a way and set straight in such a manner that the possibility of a reunion of our communions will become visible."

The best way to this development is for all of us, Catholics and Protestants, to *practice* the truth which we believe, that is to say, to live the doctrines of our Churches.

Piety

An abbot was once asked by his monks how it was possible for them to attain real unity, seeing that they were so dissimilar in origin, talents, and education. The abbot answered with a metaphor:

> Think of a wheel. It has a periphery—the rim, and a center—the hub. If we want to bring the farthest points of the rim together, they have to be moved toward the hub, as is the case with the spokes of the wheel. Similarly with us. The periphery is the world. The hub, the center, is God. The more we are trying to come closer to God, the closer we come to one another. And also the other way around: The more we cling to the "world," the more we concentrate on purely human thoughts and judgments, building on human security in a life without God, the more we move away from one another.

This is a very telling illustration for separated Christians. The center that alone can draw us together is God, the

Father of Mercy. The more we are willing, as the Apostle said, to be "led by the Spirit of God," the more we grow into Christ and thus are formed by Him, and the smaller the distance becomes between us. Very close together indeed are the saints, the perfected Christians. For in the eternal contemplation of God, at the heavenly banquet, there will no longer be Catholic or Protestant seating arrangements. Therefore, what already unites Christians of all sides in this time here on earth, is a life of faith, hope, and love—in one word, their piety. Who could quarrel with the words of the Catholic bishop who said:

> Through the grace that is operating in our separated brothers, they are closer to God— and to us—than are Catholics who are in the state of mortal sin, and in this sense a faithful and pious Protestant or Orthodox Christian belongs more profoundly to the Church than a freethinking, marginal Catholic.

And yet, even in the outward expression of piety, there are deep, open contrasts which separate Christians like veritable gulfs. To a Protestant, the Catholic devotion to Mary, for example, or to the saints may appear incomprehensible, even un-Christian, while the Catholic feels like a stranger in a Protestant church without the tabernacle, the statues of the Mother of God, or pews with kneelers. To be sure, one cannot simply speak of a Catholic or Protestant piety as though these were absolute categories. For neither here nor there can everything be brought down to a common denominator. The variety of fundamental religious experiences, a man's personal experience of God, national differences—all these elements result in diverse manifestations of piety. (Spaniards and Germans, for instance, adhere to quite different forms of piety within one and the same Catholic Church, as do the various spiritual disciplines, Jesuit and Benedictine and the rest of the endless variety of religious orders.) All this reminds us that on this subject we simply cannot generalize.

So let us leave aside these various forms of piety which are conditioned by nontheological factors, and ask what the underlying theological problems are that separate Catholics and Protestants in their basic religious positions.

A basic concern in the Protestant religious posture is the preservation of the absolute sovereignty of God. God and man, Creator and creature—these are two entirely different levels. And yet God is present to man. In the final analysis, it is in the manner in which the believer is aware of the presence of God, that religion is manifested. A Protestant theologian says quite rightly: "Protestant Christianity, as compared to Catholicism, has a different concept of the presence of God." [3]

To respect the sovereignty and absolute superiority of God in this world, the Protestant shies away from anything in the religious sphere that might tend to tie God, as it were, to His creature, to guarantee His presence. That the tabernacle is missing in Protestant churches has a deeper meaning than can be found merely in a different doctrine of the Eucharist. Protestantism denies the continuity of the apostolic office, which it sees as limited in time and replaced by Scripture. With the establishment of the scriptural canon by the Church, the place formerly filled

---

3. Hauter, "Les raisons persistantes de la division" in *Foi et vie*, 49 (1951), p. 21.

by the college of the Apostles, a community of persons, is now taken by Holy Writ. But it, in turn, may not be bound either to anything that guarantees permanency such as, for example, the teaching office of the Church.

God is not bound to any Scripture. Like any other object of historicity, Holy Scripture is subject to profane methods of interpretation. It is conceivable that someone may not find God in it. "In order for the bible to become Holy Scripture, a charismatic intervention is required. This intervention may or may not take place." [4] God in His sovereignty and superiority over this world is free to act or not to act. What profound reasoning underlies the "scriptural principle" of Protestantism! And it is this thinking that also determines the characteristic piety of our Protestant brethren. Their concern is the transcendance of God, the respect for His absolute independence from our world.

This same consciousness of distance (between God and man) also underlies the hesitation of Protestantism to make any positive assertions about man. With respect to him, only God's doing, God's salutary action can be considered. Man, considered by himself, is only a sinner, far from God. And because man is merely an object of the redeeming action of God, there is no possibility of human cooperation. God alone, Christ alone, grace alone—these are the core words which determine the piety of our Protestant brethren, however much their theology is qualifying today this "alone" of the Reformers.

The basic Catholic posture is different. The Catholic is very much aware of the difference between God and man, and the latter's dependence on God's all-pervading action.

4. Hauter, *op. cit.*, p. 19.

But he does not look at this all-pervading action as an exclusively one-sided act. When the Catholic contemplates God's redeeming work, he concentrates not only on the God who showers graces on us, but also on the gift of grace itself, and on the dignity and glory which are bestowed on man so favored by God. For the Catholic, grace is an act of God and, in consequence of this act, it is a reality within created nature, that is to say, a reality which indeed transforms the nature of the creature, and to partake of the life of God. "Already," "here and now" —these are basic Catholic terms. Here and now—God's tabernacle among men; here and now—the communion of saints. Man, therefore, is not an isolated individual but, as a Protestant theologian expressed it, "the Catholic is a person who is never alone. By means of symbols and the help of the saints, he is accompanied in his praying and living by the entire community of the faithful."[5]

In venerating Mary and the saints, the Catholic says in effect: God is not an "out-of-this-world" abstraction. He is the creator of all that is visible. And the Second Person of the Trinity has in reality become man. The Catholic, in other words, professes a God who loves what He has created and who, in the person of the incarnate Christ, has imparted Himself to the world. The Catholic believes that his love for God is genuine only when it also wants men to be as God intended them to be. We Catholics love what God loves, through His love—that is to say, not as something provisional or tentative, as a cloud in a perpetual state of flux. We love the creature as something that is valid before God, eternally justified, as something

5. P. Burgelin: "Psychologie Protestante et Psychologie Catholique," in *Foi et Vie,* Vol. 49 (1951), p. 30.

which in God's plan has religious significance (K. Rahner).

Protestant piety is characterized by features reminiscent of the Old Testament prophets. That is both its strength and its weakness. When we Catholics say "God and man," "Christ but also Mary," "grace—a favor, but also a gift that transforms man," then the Protestant suspects a polytheistic tendency. We see this time and again in Martin Luther—in his concern, for example, that Mary might be made into an idol. In his explanation of the Magnificat he writes:

> God's grace has all too lightly been put aside; this is dangerous, and it is not justified by our love for Mary. What is needed is moderation lest we go too far with her name by calling her the queen of heaven. Granted that this is true, she nevertheless is not a goddess who could bestow something or help us, as some people think who have more recourse to her than to God Himself. We may pray to her that, for her sake, God may grant us that for which we pray. But the work (the act of granting) must always remain God's alone.

It is true that Catholic piety again and again needs this prophetic correction. We must not forget that human existence is a broken existence, and that there simply is no such thing as a smooth transition from nature to grace. But Catholic piety can, when the need arises, be corrected without sacrificing its basic principles, while a correction of the basic Protestant principle seems to us impossible because it is founded on exclusiveness.

The Catholic is frequently under the impression that

Protestant thinking moves within the perspectives of the Old Testament though qualified by the event of the Incarnation with its characteristics of promise and expectation. The Catholic, on the other side, extends the incarnation of Christ into history and thus, in the eyes of Protestants, compromises the momentum of promise and eschatological expectation. It is obvious that two different concepts are here in opposition. However, the conflict is not absolute. The French Dominican Hamer wrote:

> If there actually exists a contrast between Protestant "exclusiveness" and Catholic "universalism," then the concepts used also indicate its limitations. The positive elements of Protestantism are not in conflict with the corresponding Catholic values. The dilemma takes shape only when these truths are isolated from the whole and taken out of the organic context from which they draw their vitality and in which they find their dimension.[6]

There are dangers lurking behind both these two basic religious positions, but we should be careful lest we judge each other from the point of view of these dangers. Catholic piety is not paganism, nor is it magic or a mythical goddess-cult. Nor is Protestant religious experience merely romantic natural piety or individualistic caprice, or even Godlessness. We should take each other sufficiently seriously to search for the theological backgrounds of our different positions. Concretely this means, for example, that we should begin to explore such questions as the

6. *Una Sancta*, Vol. 12 (1957), p. 191.

meaning and the consequences of the incarnation of Jesus Christ, the nature of grace, and the eschatological second coming of Christ. But we all must have the motive which St. Benedict enjoined on his monks: "That in everything God may be glorified."

Reforms

The Unity Octave, a week of prayer for the unity of all Christians, begins in January of each year with the feast of the Chair of St. Peter in Rome, and ends with the feast of the Conversion of St. Paul. Thus, all Christian efforts toward union in faith are overshadowed by the word "conversion." Some Catholics understand this to mean that the non-Catholics have to come as converts into the Catholic Church. Some Catholic prayer-texts for this week have no other intention than to pray for the conversion of the Orthodox, the Lutherans, the Anglicans, etc. In all these certainly well-meant prayers, however, one thing is forgotten: No prayers are said for the conversion of the Catholics themselves. "But what should we convert to?" we ask. "We have the truth, don't we?" What blindness!

The word "conversion" at the end of the prayer-week for unity is found in the text of the feast of St. Paul. This must mean, therefore, that we should *all* be converted, just as St. Paul was, to the Gospel of Jesus Christ. A prayer in this spirit will open to the minds of those who pray it the necessity of disposing themselves to the will of God, to surrender themselves to the plans and ways of God—which often are quite different from the way we imagine them to be. Such a prayer for our own conversion will make us look, first of all, into our own house and, if we want others to return to it, will lead us to prepare it as a house of catholicity, a house in which the Gospel of Jesus Christ will be so made known that it cannot remain unheard.

To reform the Church means more than merely to overhaul the apparatus of its organization; it means, in the final analysis, to make the real face of the Church stand out unclouded and radiant. Reform of the Church always means renewal of the inner vitality of the Church, as was done, for example, by the Council of Trent, which led to a new spiritual life in the Church. Francis de Sales, Vincent de Paul, Cardinal Berulle are but a few of the names that come to mind in thinking of renewal in the Church. Berulle particularly, who founded the French order of the Oratorians and was called the mystic of the Incarnate Word, gave us an indirect answer to the main concern of the reformers by preparing the way for a theocentric piety, a piety in which God stands in the center of all things. God does not exist for us, we exist for Him. The post-Tridentine period shows us that the genuine reformer in the Church is not the intellectual but the saint. Whenever a saint appears and God uses him to renew the religious energies of the Church, there the proper action to overcome the schism is being applied.

If we look at our time under this aspect, we may say that in the Catholic Church as well as among our separated brethren genuine reforms have become evident in a new turning to the Gospel of Jesus Christ. On the Protestant side, the rediscovery of the sacraments of Confession and Eucharist, on the Catholic side the biblical movement—

these are signs of a convergence of separated Christians. The most essential and most important ecumenical work is being done—has to be done—in one's own camp.

The council which Pope John XXIII began continues under his successor, Paul VI. It cannot yet be expected that this council will deal with the question of reunion of Christianity in such a direct manner as the Council of Florence did in the fifteenth century with respect to the Orthodox. The time for that is not yet right, it seems. But every Catholic renewal also serves indirectly the ecumenical concern by creating the atmosphere in which dialogue between the separated Christians becomes possible.

Some will ask what the significance of the Second Vatican Council can be for the Catholic Church in which the infallibility of the pope can dispose of all disputable problems. Some even ask whether the dogma of papal infallibility pronounced in 1870 did not actually make future councils superfluous. The Vatican Council which proclaimed the dogma of the pope's infallibility had this to say in the opening statement of its constitution, *Dei Filius,* on the topic of later councils:

> There the sacred dogmas of religion are being defined with greater profundity and expressed with greater ardor; the discipline of the Church is renewed; and when the members are united to the head, the vitality of the entire Mystical Body of Christ is strengthened.

Whoever studies the history of the councils knows that the cooperation of the many participants in a council always produces a much wider range of views and greater wealth of experience than the decision of a single person could reveal. The cooperation of the theologians, who on many points may be of differing opinions, always produces in the final statements of a council a purity and fullness of Catholic thought such as a single individual, however well advised, would never be able to achieve. In 1543, Cardinal Cajetan expressed a similar thought in these words: "The authority of the pope can equal that of a council in power and intensity, but never will it be equal to it in scope and concrete fullness." Someone spoke some time ago of the "more catholic Catholics" who are needed for the ecumenical task. A council will always promote this fuller Catholicity—and in this respect we may, indeed, expect progress in the current council toward overcoming the divisions of faith.

A glance into the history of the Church shows that those reforms that were prompted by pastoral concerns always had thorough-going success, not those that tended to increase the power of the Church or which created a split. In other words: The successful reforms were motivated by the charity of the Good Shepherd and were aimed at the salvation of souls. A point of special interest can be noted here: A reform always is dangerous and may even become disastrous whenever it is prompted by rationalistic or doctrinaire motives. Modernism and the theology of the enlightenment are but two such examples. Congar says wisely:

> One thing history has taught us, that the Roman Church cannot be reformed by movements such as the Enlightenment, Old-Catholicism, Reform Catholicism, or Modernism —which were all dominated primarily by rationalistic tendencies. Renewal can come only

from a deeply religious understanding and
acceptance of the whole and undiminished
idea of Catholicity, and from the ideal of
sanctity.[7]

To all reform movements in the Roman Church apply the
words of Cardinal Newman: "If we are holy, all will be
done well." In practice this means avoiding premature
solutions; in short, to have patience.

This patience is not a matter of mere inactive waiting;
it is rather a state of humility and intellectual reserve, a
harmonizing of spirit and intellect, so that the result of
our efforts will not be a premature birth of solutions incapable of life. And in this context it is also true that an
individual, or a group, especially when inspired by zeal
for reform, can easily lose sight of the whole, of the
breadth of Catholicity in its fullness.

The most effective reforms in the Catholic Church
always began on the lower levels, at the grassroots. But
it is necessary that the hierarchy keep the main channels
of reform under control, not to slow it up but in order to
channel the many small rivulets and streams into the great
Catholic current. Which of us can judge whether a particular reform which might be ideal for Germany, may not
perhaps have negative results in South America? Our non-
Catholic brethren might ponder this also whenever they
feel that the Catholic Church moves too slowly. The same
thing is true in reverse. The introduction of a new, maybe
even better, liturgy in a Lutheran Church, which would
be welcomed by us as a bridge-building element, can be
accomplished only if and when the people have been
prepared and are ready for it. Every reform must work

7. *Vraie et fausse Réforme dans l'Église*, p. 253.

itself out in a process of selection and organic adaptation and development.

In this context it is useful to recall some papal pronouncements of recent years which assimilated Catholic reform tendencies into the body of the universal Church, and which thus took on great ecumenical significance.

There is, first of all, the encyclical *Spiritus Paraclitus* by Benedict XV, issued on September 15, 1920, for the 1500th anniversary of St. Hieronymus' death. This encyclical was devoted to Holy Scripture and recommended its daily reading. Catholic and Protestant Christians reading daily in the Holy Scriptures—that would indeed be tantamount to building solid bridges for one another. The same subject was treated by Pius XII in his encyclical on "the timely promotion of biblical studies," *Divino afflante Spiritu,* of September 30, 1943. In it the pope referred to the Holy Spirit as "the most precious source and divine norm for the teaching of faith and morals," and he called for the wide dissemination and reading of Holy Scripture.

Of great ecumenical significance was Pius XII's encyclical on the Mystical Body, *Mystici Corporis,* which was issued June 29, 1943. Here, membership of the separated Christians in the Mystical Body of Christ is positively defined: "Even though unsuspectingly, they are related to the Mystical Body of the Redeemer in desire and intent." The pope rejects any form of pressure on non-Catholics to join the Catholic Church; whenever anyone against his will is compelled to embrace the Catholic faith, our sense of duty demands that we condemn the act. The encyclical prompted Catholic theologians to search ever further for the positive Christian values among the non-Catholic believers and their communities.

No less significant for the ecumenical dialogue was

Pius XII's encyclical on the sacred liturgy, *Mediator Dei,*
of November 20, 1947. In it, the centuries-old Protestant
objections against the Mass, mistakenly regarded as mere
human manipulation, are undone. For the encyclical de-
fines and shows the liturgy as the "public worship of the
Mystical Body of Christ and its members." The emphasis
in divine worship must be seen in its power to transform
man interiorly. The pope thus took issue with an empty
ritualism and formalism. The abuses of the sixteenth century are admitted (what a different atmosphere there is
among separated Christians when Catholics also confess
their guilt!) and his call is for a theocentric piety. In the
Mass, so says the encyclical, Christ Himself is the offering
priest and the victim offered. All Christians have a part in
the priesthood of Christ. Communion is an essential part of
the Mass. Do we not hear behind these words of the pope
the genuine concerns of the Reformers?

Conversely, whoever listens attentively to what is happening in the Protestant world can identify similar stirrings
of reform. The signs of hostility against the Catholic
Church are being dismantled in an effort towards a
broader, more comprehensive reception of the Gospel—as
in the question of the nature of revelation, of tradition, the
nature of the Church, Church law and Church office. The
liberal era in Protestant theology is all but past. There is a
growing demand for the monastic life. Dogma and creed
are being taken seriously again. Rigid biblicism and hu-
manistic tendencies are in the process of being overcome.
And much more is happening.

Contrasts are still deep and, humanly speaking, irreconcilable, yet it is obvious that the Holy Spirit of God is at
work. To Him let us abandon ourselves with confidence.

7

Joseph Auda

THE SIGN OF
THE DISCIPLES
OF JESUS

Oneness Through Baptism

THE TIME WHEN the members of separated Christendom referred to each other as "heretics" belongs to the past. It may be taken as a sign and as a fruit of the true change in thinking that today, in meeting with and speaking to each other, we know ourselves as *brothers*. The new and improved style in our mutual relations has been legitimized and authorized in this century of the Church, in this century of the desire for the unity of Christendom, by Pope John XXIII, the ecumenical pope himself. John, whose mission it was for years to work among those separated from the Apostolic See, personally spoke of non-Catholics as "our separated brethren." Even though we cannot ignore our "separateness," we still know ourselves united in Christ through the unifying bond of Baptism: "For in one Spirit we were all baptized into one body" (1 Cor. 12: 13).

This sacramentally founded unity demands that communication between ourselves be marked by the awareness that we all are encompassed by the redemptive action of our Lord, and that we must be witnesses to His mystical reality. This is especially necessary in a world which everywhere displays the symptoms of its secession from faith in Christ and its readiness to preach the gospel of unbelief.

Both Catholics and non-Catholics read the "Holy Gospel" of our Lord. But that requires that we take to heart, in good conscience, the word of the apostle who pondered deeply the gospel of Christ: "For all you who have been baptized into Christ have put on Christ" (Gal. 3: 27). What else can the image of "putting on Christ" mean than being one with Him? "For you are all one in Christ Jesus" (Gal. 3: 28).

It is painful and scandalous that we who are baptized are as yet unable to demonstrate the visible unity of all Christians, as Christ has willed it. It is indeed the cross of Christianity's division that the unity of Christians, founded as it is in Baptism, has not achieved its crowning seal and glory in one common table of the sacrament of the Eucharist, around which we could gather to strengthen in us the bond of unity and love. Whenever, therefore, we celebrate the mystery of the eucharistic banquet with our glorified Lord, the pain and shame of the cross of our disunity cannot but burn in us. Through the guilt of us Christians, the sacrament of union has become the mark of our separation. The banquet of the Lord does not unite us with our Protestant brothers and sisters in a visible community, because weighty and important differences in doctrine make this impossible.

The Church is one. The Christians still split in disunity should confidently strive towards visible union, whenever and however the Lord may will it. In the meantime, however, we must make ourselves ever more profoundly aware of the union which is founded in Baptism: All "who have been marked by the name Christian" have "put on Christ."

This is a mystery which transcends all created intelligence; it is the gift of God's mercy and grace, but one which—and especially among the separated brothers—must become for us challenge and task. Even in our separateness we must embrace each other as brethren, and in the truth of our oneness which we have come to see, we must each accept the other as a brother. The grace of Baptism enables as well as obliges us to this particular application of Christianity among our separated brethren.

Are there any manifestations and actions of ecumenical significance that point in this direction?

Praying Together

The powerful language of the liturgy of Pentecost praising the gathering in the Holy Spirit of those that were scattered, made possible by the impact of Divine grace—this voice has been muffled for centuries.

Of course, the mystery of Pentecost cannot very well be celebrated without awareness of the painful fact that the disciples of Jesus, to whom the Spirit of the Father and the Son had been sent, are not united. But the combined prayers of Catholics as well as non-Catholic Christians offer hope here. In the World Unity Octave, January 18 to 25, and again during the week before Pentecost, prayers rise incessantly to heaven pleading that God may have mercy on his Christians and grant that all who are baptized in Christ and who invoke Him, may again be "gathered together in one place," in a new miracle of Pentecost.

What Christians of the various denominations can do

for one another through prayer cannot possibly be over-rated, nor can it be assessed too highly how in the fellow-ship of such prayer they themselves are being changed and renewed. Whenever, even in our disunion, we unite in prayer, each inspired by the glad tidings of our Lord's word, there applies to us the Advent message of the Christian philosopher Peter Wust, written as a last testa-ment in the face of his death: "Prayer, understood as our ultimate act of submission, makes us quiet, makes us child-like, makes us objective. All *real humility* is marked by prayer. *The great things of life will be given only to those who pray.*" We grow in ecumenism to the extent that we become capable of praying in the name of Jesus.

There have been times when denominational contro-versy was stronger than the desire for brotherly ecumen-ical prayer. In times past, people prayed perhaps more against each other than for each other. Thank God, the times of polemics are past, and now is the time for prayer. This calling on God in a spirit of humility and contri-tion has brought us closer to each other and has permitted the realization to mature in us that through the change of heart which the Lord of the Gospel demands, we have to make good what our sins against each other have caused. Thus we can prove ourselves as Christians who deserve to be taken seriously.

We have a right to speak of our century as the ecumen-ical century because, though we are still "separated breth-ren," we at least pray for and even with one another "as brothers."

One recalls here, with gratitude to God, the retreats which take place every summer at the Benedictine Abbey of Niederaltaich. These retreats are an institution which,

operating under the patronage of Abbot Emmanuel Heufelder, OSB, is especially geared to taking care of the
needs of both Catholic and Protestant Christians. The
bond of fraternity which exists in this place is stronger
than divisions, and springs from the power and the depth
of prayer. When, after days of joint meditation and exchange of thoughts, the participants leave the abbey at
the end of the last prayer, they have experienced the close-
ness of the common Lord, the living fulfillment of His
words: "Where two or three are gathered together for my
sake, there am I in the midst of them" (Matt. 18, 20).
God indeed knows how to write straight with crooked
lines. The word of the psalmist is true even of the separated disciples of Jesus whenever they come together in
the love of Christ to debate for the sake of the truth:
"Behold how good it is and how pleasant, where brethren
dwell as one!" (Ps. 132, 1).

The prayer of the separated brethren for each other,
their separateness notwithstanding, is a sign of the disciples of Jesus, and it has given inspiration and a dimension
of depth to the ecumenical movement of our days. Is it
not a promising symptom that the desire to see separated
Christendom united is increasing in strength and intensity
among both Catholic and Protestant Christians, among
the Orthodox and the Anglicans? The more trustingly
Christians pray for this intention, the more will grow the
mutual conviction that the disunity of Christianity is an
offense and a shame. The fact that it is scandal and sin,
causing the name of God to be ridiculed among the pagans,
binds us together in a community of mourners and unites
us in a spiritual bond with all those who hope for the fulfillment of the Lord's words: "Blessed are they who

mourn for they shall be comforted" (Matt. 5, 4). The sorrow we feel under the shadow of Jesus' cross, by which unity and peace were brought into the world, has a propitiating and purifying power; it enables us to become one with the praying Christ Himself: "That all may be one, even as thou, Father, in me and I in thee; that they also may be one in us, that the world may believe that thou hast sent me (John 17: 21).

Because the visible unity of Christians now separated by their beliefs has become "the special call of God in this hour, and an urgent task" in a world about to "forge a common destiny and a common history based on solidarity," [1] ecumenical prayer has taken on a truly ecumenical missionary dimension and appeal.

Between Tuebingen and Rothenburg, on the former denominational border line between old Protestant Wuerttemberg and Bavaria, there stands the chapel of Wurmlingen. On the occasion of the World Unity Octave in 1961, without any special order or direction—unless one were to speak of the impulse provided by the Holy Spirit—prayer invitations were issued from this chapel. During the week of the Octave, the chapel was open daily from nine in the morning to four in the afternoon for this "Service of Atonement." Special posters made known the opportunity for Christians to join each other in ecumenical prayer in order to make manifest the sign of the disciples of Jesus.

Would that such examples of atonement and loving reconciliation might find imitators, so that in the reflective and prayerful togetherness of the separated brethren God's call to us in this our day might be answered by our love.

---

1. Fries: *Der Beitrag der Theologie zur Una Sancta* ("The Contribution of Theology to Una Sancta"), p. 10, Munich, 1959.

Special significance is of course attached to such individual ecumenical efforts when they are supported and encouraged by the respective Church authorities involved.

At the end of 1961, when the third plenary session of the World Council of Churches assembled in New Delhi, the Catholic bishops of Switzerland asked their faithful to pray for these deliberations. Here is what the Swiss bishops said: "From November 18 to December 12 of this year, the World Council of Churches will meet in New Delhi. We exhort our faithful to pray that the Holy Spirit may shed His light and power on the participants of this important congress and on all who are represented by them. If we thus pray for one another, the Lord will certainly send us His help so that we may understand each other better, serve Him better and, joined together in charity, shall more readily find Him in the truth."

If anyone wanted to translate St. Paul's praise of charity in viable contemporary terms, he could hardly find a better example than this appeal of the Swiss bishops which was followed by a similar appeal by the Dutch hierarchy.

At the end of 1961, the Archbishop of Cologne, Joseph Cardinal Frings, gave a widely noted address in Genoa on "The Council and Modern Thought." In his concluding remarks, he recalled for his audience the testimony of suffering which has been demanded of the Church in our time: "The last half of our century alone has produced more martyrs," he said, "than the entire three hundred years of the Roman persecutions of the early Christians. Should we, in the face of all this, still lament about weariness and lack of faith in the Church? That the Church is still, more than ever, the Church of martyrs, is our proof that the power of the Holy Spirit lives in her unbroken."

Remembering the pastoral words of the bishops of Switzerland, one could add to the words of the Cardinal of Cologne: That the power of the Holy Spirit is at work in the Church and at the same time in the separated Christians, is proven by the declaration of the Swiss bishops, which is one of the most remarkable ecumenical documents of our time and of the Church in Switzerland.

The same spirit which brings about these gifts of Christ prompted non-Catholic Christians to pray for the council fathers as they assembled for the Second Vatican Council. One is not hard pressed to find evidence for this fact.°

At an ecumenical seminar in Arnoldshain, an Evangelical pastor from Hamburg posed the question whether it would not be fitting that in the Evangelical churches "loud and public prayers be offered for the pope and the Council"; it would be almost unevangelical, the pastor continued, not to trust the Holy Spirit to further, through the Council, the unity of the Churches.

Pope John XXIII, in his encyclical *Humani Salutis*, appealed for a great partnership of prayer to accompany the immediate preparations for the great event of the

---

° An outstanding example of such prayer of non-Catholics for the success of the Vatican Council is that issued by the Faith and Order Commission of the Greater Portland Council of Churches. It was sent to all Protestant and Orthodox churches in Portland (Oregon) for use on World-wide Communion Sunday, October 7, 1962, and reads:

"O God, the Father of Our Lord Jesus Christ, the Prince of Peace, give us grace seriously to lay to heart the great dangers we are in by our unhappy divisions. Take away all hatred and prejudice, and whatsoever may hinder us from Godly union and concord.

"By the power of Thy Holy Spirit, vouchsafe to direct, sanctify, and govern Thy servant pope John and the Council which he has called together in Thy name that they may obey Thy will in all things. Grant that we may be united in one holy bond of truth and peace, of faith and charity till at length the whole of Thy dispersed sheep may be gathered together into one fold and may with one mouth and one mind glorify Thee, through Jesus Christ, our Lord." (Publishers' Note.)

council. How much he desired to hear the prayers of non-Catholic Christians at the council, also is unmistakeable in his words: "To this chorus of prayer we equally invite all the Christians of the Churches that are separated from Rome because the Council is to be equally for their blessing and benefit." He was indeed overjoyed by the certainty that "not a few have promised . . . to offer their prayers for a happy outcome to its deliberations."

The prayer of Christians for one another, surmounting all denominational border lines—this is the sign of the disciples of Jesus. The high-priestly prayer (John 17), focussed as it is on the oneness of the disciples, receives its importance and its impelling power from the nature of the last testament of our Lord given to us in the immediacy of His death suffered for our salvation. This prayer of the Lord from earth to heaven is reflected also, so it seems to us, in a prayer written by a Protestant student of theology who, before reaching his goal, had to surrender his life into the hands of his Creator; he wanted it read over his open grave: "Grant Thou to our Protestant and Catholic brethren that they may again attend together the Divine service. Behold the bleeding wound of our schism, O Lord, and have mercy on this Christendom scattered in fragments. Destroy the deadly poison of hate in their hearts and kindle in them the love of God, so that they may find each other again in Thy love."

Brotherly Dialogue

Wherever Christians separated from each other in faith pray for and with one another out of the realization of the misery of their condition and in sorrow for the seamless garment of the Lord rent by them, there it also is possible to speak of this misery, and how it can be overcome. It must be possible to speak in such a way that our words will come not under the judgment of the Lord, but under His promise: "Blessed are the peacemakers, for they shall be called children of God" (Matt. 5: 9).

Neither side is thinking of a worthless, easy peace to be won by interdenominational dialogue. The road to unity, after centuries of history burdened with many painful experiences, is today almost as narrow and steep as the road to heaven itself. Yet, we shall have to walk the one as well as the other in a spirit of sincere repentance and contrition which must be rooted in the love of God and love of our brothers in Christ.

In 1961, the Lutheran theologian Peter Meinhold pronounced these words over the Vatican Radio: "Encounters which heretofore were impossible have taken place. Discussions between the Churches which formerly would hardly have been thinkable, are underway." We believe it correct to say that the number of the "ecumenically-minded" is increasing at the present time. But what is more, there is among these unanimous agreement with the challenge of the Lutheran theologian quoted above: "What matters is that we serve the truth in charity, and that we get to know each other better."

"To serve the truth in charity"—this is the sign of the disciples of Jesus when they are engaged in controversy in matters of truth. Arguing in matters of truth is even commendable, according to St. Thomas Aquinas. But the arguing must be done in charity! In this context it is useful to remember the fifteenth chapter of the Acts of the Apostles.

The matter at issue in the young Church at that time was redemption and salvation. This was the question that concerned the Apostles in the Council of Jerusalem. The Church found itself faced by a crisis which had arisen from the tremendous growth of the Mystical Body of the Lord, and that in turn had been caused by the influx of the pagan world into the community of the disciples of Christ. In Antioch the crisis had come to a head: "Some came down from Judea and began to teach the brethren, saying, "Unless you be circumcised after the manner of Moses, you cannot be saved" (Acts 15: 1).* With Paul and Barnabas, who under the direction of the Holy Spirit were about to set out from Antioch to begin preaching among the Gentiles the Gospel of freedom from the Old Law, this demand caused "not little objection." *Controversy among the brethren!*

". . . they decided that Paul and Barnabas and certain others of them should go up to the apostles and presbyters at Jerusalem about this question. So they, sent on their way by the church, passed through Phoenicia and Samaria, relating the conversion of the Gentiles, and they caused great rejoicing among all the brethren. On arriving at Jerusalem they were welcomed by the church and the apostles and the presbyters, and they proclaimed all that God had done with them. But some of the Pharisees' sect, who had accepted the faith, got up and said, 'They must be circumcised and also told to observe the Law of Moses.' "

The Council of Jerusalem, under Peter as its head, had to render an authoritative and binding decision, for the demand of the Jewish converts to Christianity meant jeopardizing the missionary work and endangering the

Christian doctrine of justification. One cannot but think of the later convocations which have become known in history as "ecumenical councils," as one reads that there was "a long debate" (Acts 15: 7) in the council. The Holy Spirit is the one that is acting in these councils. This does not preclude all those present, whom the Lord has called to His service, from stating their views clearly and candidly. Thus, "they are not merely relegated to the simple role of recipients, but are admitted as contributors and partakers in the formation of dogma." [2]

In Jerusalem there were no communities of "separated" Christians represented at the council by delegates; still there were those who, in consequence of the tensions that had appeared, carried within themselves the dangerous germ of dissension. Those involved in the controversy rightly knew that they were bound to the primacy of truth, which had to be sought in communion with all the others until the synod gathered under the Holy Spirit had rendered its decision. James, speaking in the council, sided with the decision given by Peter (it is necessary to submit to the truth arrived at in the spirit of God), but his was to become the voice of charity in Jerusalem: The pagans joining the community of the disciples who love the Lord shall show consideration for the feelings of the Jewish converts to Christianity (Acts 15: 14 ff.).

How else could the work of this council be described than as a decision for the truth in charity? Standing on the firm rock of the office of Peter, the Apostles proclaimed in union with him the great commandment of love for the redemption and salvation of men.

---

2. Otto Cohausz, as quoted by R. Baumann: *Ein Allgemeines Konzil* ("A Universal Council"), p. 46, Wurzburg, 1960.

The Council of Jerusalem is the model for all later ecumenical councils. But the rules of conduct established in Jerusalem have also inspired the joint cooperation of theologians in our own time, as is evident in the inter-denominational dialogue of our day, and have thus made possible a shining manifestation of brotherliness. That our century is called not only the century of the Church, but also the century of the ecumenical movement, is due in great part to the attitude of the theologians on both sides. The great questions of theology are being treated more and more with charitable consideration of the separated brethren and in an awareness of responsibility for the preparation of the visible unity of the Church. What meaning could there be in the Secretariat for the Promotion of Christian Unity, which was instituted by the Holy Father, had not ecumenical-minded theologians of the past and the present done the work which made such an action possible, and had they not prepared the way with their own sacrifices and disappointments?

This precisely is the essence of the ecumenical spirit: Differences and opposing opinions are being laid open in the dialogue, not smothered or blurred over. The commitment to the truth commanded in the Sermon on the Mount compels us to clarify for each other our points of view and our convictions; love would only be belittled by vagueness and obfuscation. Only that kind of unity is given by the Holy Spirit which is born in the painful striving for truth; it is for this unity that the theologians with their labors would like to create the indispensable dispositions.

We can thank God that the times of theological polemics are past. In place of resentment, there is in many areas today a brotherly spirit. If we emphasize the areas of positive agreement here, rather than questions which are still disputed, this is done to point up, first of all, the historical change which without any question has taken place; it also is done to point out that a brotherly spirit must become the living conscience of the contending parties; brandishing of weapons will only bring about the gloating of the anti-Christ. We are not to pass judgment on each other. Whoever wants to contribute to truly Christian thinking with well-meant suggestions, must be assured of a Christian response. Even when a well-founded exception has to be voiced, it can be done in a brotherly fashion. "Fortiter in re, suaviter in modo," as the old Latin proverb has it. Dialogue between the Christian confessions sometimes reveals more evidence of the Holy Spirit than does controversy within one and the same Church.

The words in chapter 13 of the First Epistle to the Corinthians can serve as a guide for the examination of all our consciences: "Charity is patient, is kind; charity does not envy, is not pretentious, is not puffed up, is not ambitious, is not self-seeking, is not provoked; thinks no evil, does not rejoice over wickedness, but rejoices with the truth; bears with all things, believes all things, hopes all things, endures all things (1 Cor. 13: 4-7).

Ecumenical dialogue is possible only on the basis of ecumenical asceticism. Guidelines for this are given in the just-quoted words of St. Paul. Certainly, there will also be negative aspects in inter-confessional discussions. The truth is, however, that a change has taken place in the climate of our discussions, a change which not only does credit to those engaged in them, but which reveals the working of God's spirit. Dialogue between members of different denominations need not produce the fear that such conversations imply a betrayal of the gifts and insights given by God to one's own Church.[3] On the contrary, the objective, nonpolemical dialogue between the denominations of our day may indeed be called an event of historical significance for the Church, an event which makes us conscious of Christendom's responsibility for its disunion, and which intends to keep alive the concern of our common Lord for the *Una Sancta*—the one Church—and make this a burning concern of all Christians.

That we are permitted to witness genuine ecumenical exchanges today is certainly the fruit of humble, trusting, persevering prayer; it was in this strength that a few men endowed with ecumenical charisms, the pioneers of the ecumenical movement, took upon themselves the risk of paving the way for such contacts and thereby made a contribution to our present activities.

There is a wise guide line for such conversations across denominational borders to which a theologian of great gentleness, the late Bernhard Bartmann of Paderborn, called attention some years ago: "When both sides want nothing but the truth, then every statement of a new truth is a step forward towards the goal—if not of union itself, then at least of peaceful coexistence. . . ."

What the ideal of all theology should be, is expressed in a phrase by St. Paul, the Apostle of the Gentiles: "Practice the truth in love, and so grow up in all things in him who is the head, Christ" (Eph. 4. 15).

---

3. Cullmann-Karrer, *Einheit in Christus* ("Union in Christ"), p. 7, Einsiedeln, 1960.

Brotherly Encounter

It is only fitting that all Christians anxious for unity ask themselves the question: Are there any promising signs for this unity among the shepherds? For they are bound by the admonition in Acts 20: 28: "Take heed to yourselves and to the whole flock in which the Holy Spirit has placed you as bishops, to rule the Church of God, which he has purchased with his own blood."

This task of spiritual guardianship founded in the will of our Lord extends particularly to the aspect of the preservation of unity or its restoration; it requires a constant, patient alertness to the divine call in our time and humble obedience to the call, once heard. It is the will of God, in the words of St. Peter, that the bishops guide the flocks entrusted to them—and certainly the longing for the "one flock and one shepherd" which so forcefully has broken through the surface in the people of our Churches today, is a desire that is in conformity with the will of God. And God has indeed given us such shepherds in our days who have recognized that this is God's hour, the hour of preparation for the courageous steps that will have to be taken on the road to the Cross, the road away from the babel of disunion, and whose last station will be the pentecostal gathering of a united Christendom.

Pope John XXIII, from the first day of his pontificate on, was animated in all he said and did with the responsibility implied in the promise and the judgment of our Lord's words: "He who is not with me is against me, and he who does not gather with me scatters" (Matt. 12: 30). The Holy Father, who in the service of the Apostolic See, had lived for twenty years among the brethren in Bulgaria, in

Turkey, and in Greece, offered in the first radio address of his pontificate the kiss of peace, as it were, to all Christians of the East with these words:

"We embrace all of the Eastern Church as much as that of the West with warm, paternal affection and we include those that are separated from the Apostolic See where Peter lives in his successors even to the consummation of the world, carrying on the mandate of Christ to bind and to loose everything on earth and to tend the flock of the Lord in its entirety. To them also we open, filled with charity, our heart and our arms. We ardently wish for their return home to the house of our Father, and we repeat the words of our Redeemer: 'Holy Father, keep in Thy name those whom thou hast given me, that they may be one even as we are,' so 'there shall be one fold and one shepherd.' We pray that they all may come of their own free will. And, with the help of God, may it be soon. They will not find a strange house but their very own, that which their fathers of old illumined with their love and adorned with their virtue."

This is the language of a heart alive with the fraternal spirit of the New Testament and resolved to atone for any intention or behavior which in the past permitted the gulf between the Christian West and the Christian East to widen and to deepen.

This greeting of peace, repeated in the Pope's Christmas message of 1958, was fraternally repayed by the Ecumenical Patriarch of Constantinople, Athenagoras, in his New Year's message of 1959. In it, he assured the Pope that he was praying unceasingly for unity, and that he welcomed any sincere call for peace, "all the more, as it is fitting, when it comes from the center of Christendom, the ancient

Rome." The supreme shepherd of the respected Church of Constantinople expressed the desire, "within the framework of closer contacts with the first-born Church of the West," to bring direction and strength to the embattled world of today. The Patriarch gratefully acknowledged the "call to unity of the Churches" being issued by "His Holiness, the supreme Head of the Church of Rome whom we fraternally salute." The last sentence of Athenagoras' message spoke of the hope he placed in John XXIII "who is personally so well-known to us and is loved and revered in our lands."

When Archbishop Jacobus was appointed representative (Exarch) of the Patriarch for North and South America, he paid a private visit to the Holy Father. Three hundred and sixty years had passed since a bishop of the Greek Orthodox Church had made such a contact. John XXIII instructed Msgr. Testa, his Apostolic Delegate in Turkey, to pay a return visit to the Ecumenical Patriarch in Constantinople. The Patriarch received the representative of the pope "with great joy and cordiality."

Such welcome contacts and remarkable expressions are signs of the catharsis and the change of heart which have been brought about by the Spirit of God. To the degree that separated Christians will understand and meet each other as brothers in Christ, to that degree they will make themselves and their message worthy of belief. The language which John XXIII and Athenagoras were speaking to each other is the language of the Good Shepherd who desires to gather and to unite. And precisely because the negative, destructive spirit of the adversary of God is not asleep, but is always on guard, the brotherly encounter of the chief shepherds is of providential significance.

The recognition of the significance of love as the sign of the disciples of Jesus is on the increase. And side by side with the rapprochement in words go the meetings of persons.

It was an historic event when on December 2, 1960, the Anglican Archbishop of Canterbury, Dr. Geoffrey Fisher, now retired because of age but then one of the six presidents of the World Council of Churches, paid a courtesy call on Pope John XXIII and conversed for an hour with him. We still read today with a feeling of gratitude the Anglican report of that meeting: "His Holiness expressed to the Archbishop his great desire to strengthen the brotherly feelings among all men and especially among all Christians, and the Archbishop confirmed from his own knowledge and experience, how strong and widespread is the wish of many Churches to act accordingly." There was no discussion of union between the pope and the former Anglican primate, the first one since the break with Henry VIII to attempt such a contact. According to a remark made by the pope, the conversation at this memorable meeting did not go beyond the threshold of the problems, but the intention of the Anglican dignitary coincided with that which is being followed by the Secretariat for the Promotion of Christian Unity. Union of spirit and of charity—that was the guiding star under which this visit took place.

The brotherly manner in which contact has been established among responsible leaders of the Christian communities is a manifestation of the great wave of desire for unity which has broken forth. At the same time, it is an encouragement to Christian people everywhere to cultivate, despite occasional set-backs in the day-to-day con-

tacts with their separated brethren, their particular gift of
the Holy Spirit: to hope even against hope. Those who
hope because they believe, are God's tools for ecumenical
miracles in this life.

It was a welcome piece of news that shortly before the
World Council of Churches assembly in New Delhi, the
Archbishop of Vienna, Cardinal Koenig, paid a visit to the
Ecumenical Patriarch Athenagoras. The cardinal made
the flight from Rome to Constantinople after a special
audience with the Holy Father. This visit, too, was symbolic. It was as though the Bishop of Rome, through one
of his brother bishops, extended his hand, and it was also
intended as an answer to the closing message of the
Orthodox bishops' conference in Rhodes. Here is some of
what the Orthodox bishops said in their message:

"The image of the Church renewing itself on this earth
rises resplendently in the union of charity, in that it is
fulfilling the new law (John 13:14). Through the Holy
Spirit, the Church preaches the Gospel on this earth,
namely the Peace of Christ, and fulfills the ministry of
reconciliation, as Paul, the divinely inspired Apostle of the
Nations states" (2 Cor. 5: 18). Towards the end of the
message we find the moving words: "Strengthened by the
prayer and the blessing of our Churches, our hierarchies,
and our people, whose pious spirit we represent, we greet
in charity our brethren of the venerable East to whom we
have been bound for centuries by old and unalterable ties
of spiritual kinship, and the brethren of the West with
whom we have never ceased to cooperate, remembering
the commandment of Our Lord 'that all may be one.' For
the fulfillment of this promise, our Holy Church has never
ceased to pray."

We are witnessing indeed a great moment: Confronted by a militant atheism and the missionary awakening of the non-Christian religions, the shepherds of the Christian Churches of the West and of the East feel impelled by the Apostle's command to "fulfill the law of Christ and bear one another's burden."

That under John XXIII the Roman Church became again "the first in the bond of charity" (Ignatius of Antioch) and that she intends to be and ever more become just that, is a fact of great new significance. We may interpret it as an act of reconciliation and as the outstretched hand of the pope that in 1961, on his personal initiative, Catholics participated in the Third Plenary Session of the World Council of Churches in New Delhi. Seven observers and twelve Catholic journalists, mostly priests, were welcomed with kindliness and in a spirit of friendship by Dr. Visser 't Hooft, Secretary-General of the World Council of Churches. The Holy Father had no better instruction for such occasions than the one repeatedly quoted: "Stand for *the truth in charity*." Before the plenary session had come to an end, the atmosphere had developed such cordiality that the Catholic observers were able to give three receptions in the Jesuit College St. Xavier in New Delhi. The one arranged in honor of Archbishop Ramsey, the current Anglican Primate, was attended on the Roman Catholic side by the Archbishop of Delhi, Joseph Fernandez, and his suffragan.

It is our hope that such mutual encounters of the Christian shepherds, motivated by Christian love, may increase in the future to further the cause of reconciliation. How much more convincing would the Christian message be, if it were possible to say even of the separated Christians and their shepherds: "See how they love one another."

Brotherly Action

The spirit of understanding and charity which has produced action both on the part of theologians and on the highest ecclesiastical level, must also create a bond among our communities. Christians of all the major confessions have an open ear for ecumenical concerns and a great interest in them—more so than some would consider possible.

A mass of evidence from the most diverse areas of life can be compiled to prove the correctness of the statement which Archbishop Jaeger made in his book on the Ecumenical Council: "In spite of all our disunity, there exists consensus on one point: *All are in search for the union intended by Jesus Christ.*" In the face of such a situation ecumenical pastoral care is the answer, the action which our age needs. The times when those who preached the glad tidings of the Word, the Love Incarnate, would hold themselves aloof from those who held different beliefs, as from heretics, must once and for all be a thing of the past. John XXIII, and Paul VI after him, compel us by their own example to treat members of other Christian confessions as *brothers:* "Whether they want it or not, they *are* our brothers." Only then will they cease to be our brothers when they cease to pray: "Our Father."

Ecumenical events which further the process of getting to know one another and which provide us with a chance to practice charity toward each other should be part of any pastoral work that wants to be related to the times in which we live. And these things must take place in the same atmosphere of fraternity in which clergymen of the major Christian confessions meet to exchange views with the accomplishment of common tasks in mind.

The required fidelity to principle and necessary discussion in matters of truth notwithstanding, ecumenical leadership must become a matter of course for our congregations today. No house of God should be built without its stones being consecrated by our fervent prayers for the separated brethren and for a creative peace among the various Christian denominations.

The working of the Holy Spirit cannot be arrested. Wherever it finds the ground prepared, precious fruits will result. One such fruit undoubtedly is "Oscar Cullmann's Proposition" (is it is referred to in ecumenical literature). Cullmann is a professor of New Testament exegesis and ancient Church history at the universities of Basel and Paris. His "proposition" is presented in a small booklet intended for wide circulation and titled *Catholics and Protestants—A Proposal for the Realization of Christian Solidarity.* In Switzerland, France, and Holland, to a somewhat lesser extent in Italy and Spain, and lately, also in the United States of America, Cullmann's initiative has created a great deal of good. What this theologian suggests may be helpful in implanting the idea of the unity of Christians into the consciousness of a widening circle of Christian people.

The distinguished scholar and historian points out how impossible it is to "bring about by ourselves the unity of the Churches on an ecumenical basis." He emphasizes therefore all the more the very real possibility of "working effectively for a brotherly spirit among all Christians, for a Christian solidarity." He gratefully states that in discussions among theologians even "where they cannot but admit a deep disagreement," the spirit of fraternity continues. "This spirit of fraternity exists," he asserts, "and it means much."

Cullmann's book is intended to help extend this brotherly spirit to people of all Churches. He is concerned "that we do not make a cold war hot, now that we theologians have made peace amongst ourselves." In order to strengthen such Christian solidarity, he makes the following concrete proposal. The joint prayer of separated Christians during the World Unity Octave in January (in some countries the week before Pentecost) should be given special significance through a joint fraternal *action:* a mutual collection to be taken up by both Catholics and Protestants —a collection by Protestants for poor or needy Catholics, and a collection by Catholics for poor or needy Protestants.

The idea for this proposal came to Cullmann, the biblical scholar, through the New Testament, specifically by the mention in Acts of the institution of a collection for the poor of Jerusalem by the early Church. "This tradition had an ecumenic character, for according to Galatians 2: 9 it was to unite the peacefully separated missions of the Jewish and the Gentile Christians."

To avoid misunderstanding, the author stresses that "the transplantation of this idea to our situations can of course be only by way of analogy." There was at that time no schism in the early Church. Even the distinction between the "Jewish Christian" and the purely "Gentile Christian" communities does not reflect actual reality as it existed. "The point at that time was to manifest through the symbol of a collection that in spite of all differences the Church would remain one, that those differences could therefore not become elements of dissension. Thus, the collection became a sign of solidarity, of the fraternity of all who invoke the name of Christ."

8

YVES CONGAR, OP | # WHAT THE LAITY CAN DO FOR REUNION

A MOVEMENT INSPIRED by the Spirit of God is at work in the world today. Christians—that is, those who want to submit their lives to Jesus Christ as we have come to know Him through the Apostles—have been separated by history, but now are intent on ending the scandal of their opposition and, if possible, of their division itself. For if there is *one* Lord, *one* salvation, then there also must be *one* Church—which is not at all the same as uniformity. There are legitimate differences of rights, customs, even of theological formulations of the same profound faith. That is why since the beginning of Christianity there has been an Eastern and a Western Church which have been very different from each other yet the same in fundamentals.

The ecumenical movement ("ecumenical" is derived from a Greek word meaning "world-embracing") is the sum total of the various endeavors which have as their goal the reunion of Christians in the unity of one Church. A part of these efforts is directed by the World Council of Churches in which the Catholic Church is not represented.

While in the past the two sides have quarrelled, condemned, banned, and sometimes even cruelly killed each other, today the first concern is to *understand* the old accusations; for many of them were of a serious nature and some were justified. Through a thorough search for the truth and by attempting to enter into a dialogue with all those who strive for a similar goal, an effort is being made to reach the point where in undiminished loyalty we can stand as one before Him whom we all profess as Lord, and also before the legacy He has left us in His covenant.

If today we are seeking to meet rather than to reject each other, does that mean that our love of truth or our beliefs have become lukewarm? Not at all. The irenic or ecumenical disposition springs from the same love of truth as did that other attitude which not long ago led us to intolerance. But this love now has quite different results. Until recently we insisted only on the *letter* of orthodoxy and would not admit that any truth could exist outside of it. Doubtless, no Catholic can subscribe to the opinion that dogma contains error or that heresy is truth. But we know today that this point of view, true as it is, does not exhaust the truth. If we are open to the truth regardless of where it may be found, this has nothing to do with liberalism nor with any sceptical or relativistic attitude. We know, however, that any truth can always be explained more completely and more lucidly. But how? By eliminating, as far as possible and with the purest intentions, the reasons both sides have for not coming together, and by examining honestly doctrinal opinions which, in the light of Divine revelation, appear to the other side as foreshortened or misinterpreted.

This may seem to make reunion the exclusive concern of experts, leaving nothing for the layman to do. There is certainly some truth in this objection, although many laymen excuse themselves too easily with the argument that they cannot be well versed in theological matters.

The level of education in our complex society is rising, and with an increase in understanding comes an increase in responsibility. Christians in this society must be intellectually awake, that is they must be able to put their talents to meaningful uses. There is no doubt that mature Christians today have a consciousness of their responsibilities and a willingness to master their time in a Christian sense. They want to belong to God, but in a way that does not prevent their belonging to the world also. They want a spirituality that is not suspended between heaven and earth but which embraces concrete action—a spirituality which enables them to place this activity in the hands of God.

For a Christian of today to master his times means to be useful in a society which is no longer that of the Middle Ages where everything was regulated almost as in a monastery. We live in a fragmented society devoted to technology, a society the foundations of which were determined by the French revolution and the Communist revolution of 1917, by colonialism and its exploitation of subject areas. In addition, this society has been given its impress by the Reformation. We must bear in a Christian spirit the fact of the divisions among us, even as we work and pray to end these divisions.

The work for reunion requires—as does every effort for the restoration of peace—that *everyone* be interested in it. Members of a group working for the same end are obligated to each other. The behavior of any one member of the group, especially if it gives rise to criticism, will be charged to the group as a whole. Time and again it has happened that the most promising efforts for peace were destroyed by a single unfriendly word or gesture. Conciliatory declarations which our Protestant friends would be willing to accept can still fail in their effect through the attitude of one Catholic whose Catholicism consists more of external observance than of faith—the attitude, after all, against which the Reformation protested. I recall once giving a talk to an audience of Protestants who obviously accepted my remarks as the sincere expressions of a Christian, even though they were thoroughly "Catholic" in substance. The effect of my lecture was ruined, however, by some well-meaning but misguided Catholics who stood at the rear of the hall and distributed to those leaving some pietistic literature of the kind most likely to offend Protestants.

What happened that evening is repeated every day in a variety of ways. The entire Church is responsible for the ecumenical effort. Apparently unimportant as the actions of the individual Catholic may seem to be, they are nonetheless very real. In order to make peace, we surely need specialists: diplomats and experts. But the work of the experts and diplomats would lead to nothing if they were not supported by the will and the hope of the nations. What good would any pact be if the nations wanted to go on making war? In the same way, the whole Church must take part in the ecumenical effort, just as the whole Church is interested in the missionary and reforming efforts of the Church. All must work together with the ecclesiastic superiors and specialists on whose shoulders lies in a very special way the burden of this work.

So each of us must do something. But what? What can *I* do for reunion?

Changing the Climate

Cardinal Newman relates that as a child he saw in the streets of London French prisoners of war from the battle of Waterloo marching past. He stepped down from the sidewalk and lifted the coat of one of the soldiers to see if he really had a tail. The little boy who had written in one of his school books "anti-Christ" alongside the word "pope," believed that all papists had tails. One could tell many similar stories, and some would not date back much later than yesterday or the day before yesterday. An eighty-year-old Protestant lady who is a great friend of my family, not long ago said: "It is no longer as it used to be. When I was a child I was, I believe, the only Protestant girl in my village. The other children made jokes about me. Today, however, people have respect for each other and are often genuinely fond of one another."

It is good to hear such words. But, as in all human affairs, everything has two sides. The good is always mixed with the not-so-good.

A friend, a priest in a town where the population is strongly Protestant, told me recently that he had to remind one of his parishioners who had married in the Evangelical Church of the requirements of canon law on the marriage of Catholics. But the man's wife remarked: "I thought since our pastor and the evangelical pastor now get along so well, these things don't matter any more." And when I repeated this incident to an evangelical pastor, a friend of mine in a completely different part of the country, he replied: "I had a similar case with exactly the same argument."

This will not keep us from seeking peace with our brothers, but it shows that opening up relations which manifest themselves in esteem and in dialogue, must be accompanied by a parallel education of the faithful. This will have great value. But much more remains to be done. We bear a terrible burden of wrongs. It is important that we face up to this fact unequivocally; for in the realm of psychology the discovery and identification of sickness is already the beginning of the cure.

We must come to a clear understanding of these things: The Church in the past has seldom taken positions *exclusively* as a church, but nearly always as a social organization, as Christendom—that is to say, as a society that has been a part of the West for many centuries, intimately bound up with particular customs, forms, and expressions which have come to be accorded respect, esteem, even certain prerogatives. As we all know, we have, without being conscious of it, carried all this with us into the mission countries, and thus have brought Christianity to those countries in such a manner that today, when they challenge European influence, they also challenge the Church.

As far as our relations with the separated Christians are concerned, we face them conditioned by a past which has produced in us certain forms of thinking and certain reactions. But "the others" have a past, too. We do not understand each other. Even more: In the confusing history of our past there have been rivalries and enmities on both sides, sometimes bloody wars, intolerance, and indefensible methods. How we have tried to destroy each other! The spectacle of these conflicts—the Thirty Years' War in Germany, the religious wars in France and England—is, historically speaking, one of the main causes of modern disbelief. The religions, the Christian religion not excluded, have appeared as institutions producing dissension and division and bringing about intolerance and violence. So, guidance for peace and unity was sought elsewhere.

All this is the reason why we see and address each other only through distorted ideas, habits, prejudices, and emotions. For more than twenty years the ecumenical movement has been studying all these phenomena under the heading of "nontheological factors of disunity." The phrase covers those habits of thinking passed along by history, those collective attitudes which, although they are never counted in the enumeration of our doctrinal differences, are at least as disruptive as these differences themselves. They cause the existing mutual disparity to harden into mutual annoyance.[1] It can even happen that

---

1. The concept of these nontheological factors had already been discussed at the ecumenical conferences of 1937, was especially studied in Bossey, Switzerland, in November, 1951, and then at the conference in Lund, in August, 1952. Here is a summary report of the Bossey conference findings, taken from P. M. Villain:

   1. *Factors which have caused schisms:*
     a) The development of isolated churches;
     b) Coercion or persecution by church and state (lack of freedom);
     c) Discrimination (certain groups within a church were slighted or excluded for social, economic, political, or racial reasons);
     d) The separation or expulsion of "reformers" or "innovators";
     e) The reactions caused by plans for reunion;
     f) National hostilities, wars;
     g) Enmities and competition among individuals.
   2. *Factors which prolong schisms:*
     a) The existence at the present time of the factors enumerated under 1 (above);
     b) The memory of these factors which remains a self-justification for existing schisms;
     c) The psychologically founded tendency to accept the existing situation instead of questioning it;

these factors can have a more lasting effect than differences of doctrine, that they are indeed the true mainsprings of our mutual disagreements. Where the causes of disunity are doctrinal, they are reinforced by the powers of instinct and of passion, and backed up by the influence of each side's "esprit de corps." This is the case, for example, in the opposition between the Eastern and Western Churches.

The non-theological motives often have the greater influence the less strong and personal religious convictions are. We know Protestants who never attend a church and who do not even know the name of their pastor, but they can

---

d) The inaccurate presentation of other churches by press, radio, etc.;

e) The teaching of history in the schools;

f) New factors within the church (the gradual blending with social, economic and political groups; the symbolic importance of the denominational *name* and everything connected with it; the burden of an administration which tends to claim everything for itself; liturgical customs; ignorance);

g) Certain aspects of international denominational organizations (e.g. the young churches that do not feel at home in the Western ecumenical movement).

3. *Nontheological factors which underline the necessity of union:* Certain aspirations of the modern world press for union, but not necessarily true unity. The modern world favors organizations on a grand scale and much centralization. As a consequence, states issue misleading appeals to the Churches in order to be able to control them more effectively, and it can become the duty of the Church to resist this pressure. But it is no less true that the character of their unity is thereby expressed. Social grievances are a factor which could hasten union. Besides, new tasks in preaching are facing the Church (change of political boundaries, population movements); there is the opposition of the state, and persecution; the fight against state monopoly in the field of education, public health, charity (fields in which formerly the Church alone was active); the problems of the Churches in the mission lands as these countries gain their independence; etc.

think of nothing more horrible than to become a Catholic, marry a Catholic, or to raise children as Catholics. A Protestant mother said to her daughter who became a Catholic: "I would have preferred that you had become Jewish; it would have humiliated you less." [2]

Often the deeply rooted determination to have no contact with the other assumes the role of both motive and meaning of the disassociation itself. This happens frequently in human relations, and it is the case in many differences of opinion. Two people have quarrelled over a trifle, have hurt each other, but the incident has not been mentioned anymore. A long period of time passes without the two having the same opinion on anything, since they no longer exchange any friendly words or deeds. What has happened is that the one simply does not see the other any more; from this point it is only a step to mutual distrust or recrimination.

The grave consequence of such a state is the generation of a certain number of complexes, most destructive of which is that of mistrust. This is so, perhaps, because there are certain connections between the two hurts: the hurt suffered and the mistrust evoked. Mistrust anchors itself deeply in a man's heart, and is as obstructive as the feeling of injustice, coloring all our judgments. Under such circumstances all attempts to reach the other are vain; equally vain are all suggestions for a really just and generous solution to mutual difficulties. If trust is lacking, even the best intentions are suspected as a particularly clever piece of

---

2. The motive which since the nineteenth century was called the "superiority of the Protestant peoples" plays in my opinion an important role. It appears rather openly in recent publications, e.g., by Fr. Hoffet in France, who does not enjoy any great prestige even with Protestants, and by Paul Blanshard in the United States.

cunning, if not worse. How often we have had such experiences, which undoubtedly can be duplicated by similar ones encountered by Protestants and Orthodox. Twenty times an explanation proposed by us has been rejected, has not even been understood; our way of interpreting a certain text has been rejected. But as soon as we quoted a passage from Luther or Calvin, or from one of the Greek Fathers of the Church which said exactly the same thing, there was immediate consent. Then "the others" felt secure.

A further reason why the Christian life today demands more than ever insight and understanding, is found in the fact that this life requires confrontation and dialogue; but one can venture into these areas only if one is well trained. Time and again, F. Mersch's word is borne out: "In the absence of a skeleton, certain animals must put on armor."

Among the complexes which "the others" often have in regard to us (in close conjunction with the mistrust just mentioned) is the famous anti-Rome complex; with certain distinctions in reasoning and expression, this complex seems to be common to the Orthodox East as well as the Protestant West. This attitude is a profound fact, whether or not it is a Christian attitude. I by no means exclude the possibility that in its deepest meaning this attitude finds a kind of justification in its adherence to true Christian values, even though these are sometimes misunderstood. In my opinion, one could find a formulation of these values as well as their questionable interpretation in Dostoevski's Legend of the Grand Inquisitor in *The Brothers Karamazov*. I had been a priest for exactly a year when, within a period of a few weeks, both a

Protestant pastor in Berlin and an Orthodox friend in Paris referred me to this passage by Dostoevski, as though to express through it the essential point of their own indictment of the Roman Church.

We Catholics, from the pope to the last layman, cannot but bear this in mind. It would only be proper if Rome humbly, sympathetically, and honestly were to inquire into the reasons for this disturbing state of affairs that persists stubbornly in thousands of facts and texts throughout history: the Catholic Church is not loved; it is mistrusted. It is accused of wanting to rule, to dominate—and this is why people keep aloof from it and seek to protect themselves against it. Almost all the most solemn papal documents begin with a long paragraph in which the popes say that they have done everything they could and should have done; it is the world which is evil and has not listened. But the only one who believes this is Rome, even though many people outside the Catholic sphere are willing to recognize the good deeds that have come from the papacy for Christianity and for the world. If we would approach such problems honestly and truthfully, especially if those in authority would consider them, the atmosphere would be cleared, just as after a thunderstorm in summer one breathes clear air again.

But once again: What can lay people do?

Much. Even speak, if the occasion arises. There are after all practical occasions where we can cooperate to clear the complexes away—the mistrust, the lack of contact, the nontheological factors of our separation—in order to achieve that change of climate which, thank God, has already begun.

The Habit of Mutual Respect

This must begin with the education of children. I am of the opinion that it is of great benefit to Catholic children to have Protestant and Jewish playmates and friends. If the Christian atmosphere at home is healthy and reasonable, these mixed friendships do not harbor any danger of syncretism (intermixture of doctrines) or religious liberalism; on the contrary, they have the great advantage of introducing the children to a fundamental disposition of Christianity today, that of openness to mutual dialogue.

In our educational efforts toward an understanding of "the others" we must direct attention to another important point: the way we speak about them. Without being conscious of it, adults transmit spiritual attitudes. If I use derogatory names for people of other faiths, I thereby channel my thoughts into a direction which implies deprecation. It is probable that the image I form of others and the image in which I see them will look the same. Propaganda uses such images and expressions to great effect. The language in our school books should be carefully watched as must the expressions we ourselves use in our daily conversations.

Getting to Know Each Other

All Catholics who work for unity today began by seriously educating themselves in the subject. At the present time, we have Catholic magazines that specialize in this field and publish excellent reports on the ecumenical movement, as well as general-interest Catholic magazines which also carry good occasional articles on the subject.

The reliable information these sources furnish about "the others" has often been praised by the latter.

It is indispensable to have reliable fundamental knowledge about the Eastern Church, the Reformers, and present-day Protestantism. The annual observation of the Unity Octave provides an occasion to make such information available to parishes and schools through lectures, distribution of pamphlets, press notices, and parish bulletins, possibly also through exhibitions, and perhaps in such a way that every day, in connection with the prayer intention of the octave, a brief explanation will be given on a different aspect of the subject: the Eastern Church, the main branches of Protestantism, the ecumenical movement, the missions, etc.

Opportunities for Spreading Understanding

It is obviously very difficult to assess one's own viewpoint as opposed to that of another. Everyone is a bad judge in his own cause. It is not to be recommended, then —in fact rather the contrary—that Catholics at every opportune and inopportune time pose as world reformers ready to clear up controversial theological issues once and for all. In doing this, we only would draw down hatred on ourselves and would in time accustom ourselves to a narrow and rigid intellectual attitude. We could come to presume that there are no truths at all outside those known to us as Catholics, and we would thus become incapable of accepting anything else. Such an attitude would not be Christian. We should always strive to avail ourselves of the truth and live in the continuous disposition to mend our ways. And indeed, in every dialogue we receive at least as much as we contribute. If the occasion demands, we also shall have to know how to correct a wrong interpretation quietly yet emphatically; how to explain a stand our Church takes and to show her true face—to show the truth not recognized by our partners in the conversation; how to refer them to this or that book or article, or to a lecture which might have a clarifying, pacifying effect. In all this, the most we shall be seeking is an opportunity for *positive* explanation, definitely avoiding argumentation that might lead to controversy. It is better to build stone by stone than to unload a truck full of stones all at once at the risk of burying someone beneath the pile.

Building Bridges

There are many opportunities for cooperation in the field of charity, in help for distressed or underdeveloped areas; cooperative endeavors in union activities, civic, or political affairs; or cooperative actions of protest or opposition against measures which violate the demands of the Christian conscience. There are indeed many possibilities of encounter in areas where we can act together as Christians in spite of some certainly substantial differences in our dogmatic concepts; occasions where, while retaining our own viewpoints and without denying them, we can nevertheless appreciate the genuine Christianity of "the others." On this basis we should search tirelessly for a consensus which denies nothing of the sacred treasure of truth but which aims at the perfecting of that which—though still scattered—is already in existence here and there.

Prayer for Reunion

Prayer forms the Christian, for it is the breathing of the soul which has surrendered itself in faith to the living God. The prayer of Christians, individually or corporately, forms a center of love in which souls are sustained in the community of the saints. The work of the Church, as every Christian work, is a *spiritual* work. It does not proceed from the world of human enterprise and its economy, but from cooperation with a merciful God who wants to save man. Spiritual work is not the result of human diplomacy. What diplomacy can contribute by way of discussion and negotiation is only the human aspect; these disciplines are *real* and necessary of course, but neither the profoundest nor the most decisive of features. Things spiritual can neither be accepted nor brought into being unless it be through the Holy Spirit. The fruit of unity can come only from Him who, without violating consciences, can turn them interiorly in the direction of unity. All the more is this true for this unbelievable miracle: the concord of Christians, separated as they are by contradictory beliefs, all trying with the utmost religious fidelity to preserve what has been handed down to them by their fathers and their Church.

Prayer is effective, for it fulfills a condition which God expects from us in answer to His grace, in order to carry out His plan of salvation for us. It does not "change" the designs of God but it coincides with what He expects of us, so that His will may be done on earth, in human history, as it is in heaven. St. John Chrysostom wrote: "The man who prays has his hand at the helm of the world." How much more must that be true in the prayer "that all may be one" which, harking back to the intent and text of John (Chapter 17), is one with the prayer of Jesus Himself.

We do not always receive what we ask in our prayers, or at least not in the way we imagine or desire it. But there is one fruit of prayer which is always certain: a change of heart. We are never the same when we have finished a prayer as when we began it. When others are united to us in prayer, whether we are praying with them or for them, our relationship to them is profoundly altered. The prayer *for* another, for an "enemy," or for a person who has wronged us, opens our heart in a way which would not have been possible without such a prayer. Prayer *with* a person establishes first-hand contact, opens eyes, dissolves mistrust.

Time and again I have had this experience in meetings with Protestants and with Orthodox. Prayer was not a substitute for the confrontation of doctrine, but it enabled this confrontation to unfold in a less argumentative climate, which in turn allowed us to reach a more profound spiritual depth, and rooted us in the confidence and in the intent that we were called to do something together.

The joint prayer of Christians who belong to different confessions is naturally subject to certain rules. These rules are not the outcroppings of chicanery and narrow-mindedness; the official rules of the Catholic Church in this respect are even remarkably generous. What must be safeguarded is the fidelity of each person to his own Church. And it is also a question of being honest in the face of schism, a matter which must be faced in all its unfortunate consequences.

Rules for Prayers with Others

In normal circumstances a Catholic is not permitted to participate actively in a public Divine Service of a community of another faith; in practice that means the celebration of the sacraments, and especially the Eucharist. Doing so would entail the sin of *communicatio in sacris* (*in divinis*)—participation in the liturgical community.

Two phrases in this text need explaining:

1. "In normal circumstances." This is important because the Church permits, in danger of death, if a Catholic priest cannot be found and the twofold danger of imperiling the person's faith and of scandal to others is not present, a Catholic to receive sacramental absolution and communion from a priest of a schismatic Church (whose priesthood is valid). It appears that in the face of death (in theological language the situation would be described as *eschatological),* the rules of law lose some of their importance. The demand of the Church yields to the spiritual welfare of the man who is about to enter eternity, that is to say, that state which is final, and in the face of which all regulations of the Church have only one function—to serve.

2. "Participate actively." This means to behave exactly like a member of the other Christian community. One may do so only when one is in fact a member of that community. To act like a member without being one would be a lack of fidelity toward one's own communion or Church, for one would be enacting the ecclesiastical or liturgical rite of another Church, and that would be something like spiritual adultery. At the same time a person

would do a wrong against the other community by participating in an act of that community without belonging to it.

Nevertheless, the section of canon law which regulates the behavior of Christians outside a church does permit in certain cases the participation in public Divine Services of other faiths. In such instances "passive" attendance is required. What does this mean? It does not mean that one is not allowed to pray, still less that an attitude should be assumed which would be offensive to the members of the cult one is attending; then it would be better to stay at home. "Passive attendance" only means that one should not participate in the public acts of such a service, as the others do who are members of that Church. Such situations are justified, for instance, when an important occasion in the family requires such a presence, and one's position demands it, e.g., attendance at a Baptism, a wedding, or a funeral. When in doubt, the bishop (or the chancery office) should be consulted. (Canon Law 1258, S. 2.)

I believe that ecumenical studies or participation in ecumenical meetings can, under the usual conditions, be counted among these important occasions, provided that neither the danger of scandal nor that of defection exists (two conditions which are justified by the warnings of Jesus against giving scandal: see Matthew 5: 29-30, and 18: 6-9).

But simple curiosity could not be considered sufficient justification. Nor is a Catholic permitted to act as a godparent in the liturgical meaning of the word at a non-Catholic Baptism, or as a witness at a non-Catholic wedding.

It should be clearly understood that these prohibitions are not motivated by a mean or suspicious spirit. These are occasions when the Christian feels very keenly the burden of separation which he has to bear, and in the light of this tragedy, he must give a spiritual explanation for his attitude. It is best in such cases simply to decline the invitation with a frank but proper explanation, expressing fully the regret we feel at being obliged to refuse.

While the Church is strict in the entire sphere of official ecclesiastical acts, that is to say in regard to Divine Service, she permits on the other hand Christians to pray together on the level of private life. "Private" in this context does not mean secret, within four walls; it means nonliturgical, that is to say, apart from the liturgical Divine Service which is public service. Thus it is permissible to pray together aloud at a gathering such as a study circle or a lecture. The encyclical *Ecclesia Catholica* of December 20, 1949, which formulates the norms to be observed on such occasions, expressly permits the joint recitation of the Lord's Prayer (the Our Father), or of any other Church-approved prayer such as the psalms, or even of a prayer from the missal, as long as it is outside of a liturgical action. This is being done frequently at ecumenical gatherings even under the chairmanship of our bishops, at the various observances of the Unity Octave, at the end of an address, etc. Such prayer, generally experienced with profound feeling, is not only very impressive; one cannot doubt that God will hear it: "Where two or three are gathered in my name...."

The Unity Octave

The Unity Octave, as it is generally known, is being observed all over the world from January 18 to 25 each year. In the Catholic calendar, this is from the feast of the

Chair of St. Peter in Rome to the feast of the Conversion
of St. Paul—feasts which obviously are full of ecumenical
meaning. The sequence of the two feasts also appears to
be of importance. The concluding feast celebrates a conversion which is not intended as a symbol for the conversion of non-Catholics to the Catholic Church, but primarily
as a symbol for the return of *all* to the spirit of the Gospel.

This week of prayer, now called the World Unity
Octave, was initiated in 1908 by two Anglican clergymen,
Spencer Jones and Paul Wattson, who founded in the
United States a community under the name of the Society
of the Atonement (meaning simultaneously redemption,
expiation, and reconciliation). In the same year, 1908,
Father Wattson became a Catholic.

This prayer week was especially promoted by Popes
Pius X, Benedict XV, and Pius XI. Before that, there had
been already in existence a novena for the reunion of
Christians which was held between the feast of the Ascension and Pentecost; it had been introduced by Leo XIII.
The Unity Octave in January, however, soon won out over
the Pentecost novena, not only because it could be held
at a time which is relatively free for lectures and meetings,
but also on the strength of its original idea, which was
greatly advanced by Father Paul Couturier, who died
March 24, 1953.

The Unity Octave was originally intended for Catholics
and those friendly to the Catholic Church who would
devote themselves to prayer for the return of Christians
belonging to the various Christian denominations, and also
for fallen-away Catholics. Each day had a special prayer
intention, a fact that served as a practical framework for
a series of addresses. But it was not intended to narrow

or to limit these prayers; the intent was rather to include the entirety, or better the *oneness* of an undivided concern for Christian unity. Besides, when prayer is a real act of faith, it does not need any particular specialization, as do the forms of veneration or reparation; it is incorporated into the totality of the Divine plan.

Since the main purpose of the Unity Octave was to pray expressly and particularly for the return of the separated brothers to the Catholic fold, we obviously could not expect the Anglicans, the Protestants, and the Orthodox to join us in this world week of prayer. But the Unity Octave in January became more and more an occasion where separated Christians, while yet being unable to pray in unison, in one Church, could continue to beseech God unceasingly, simultaneously, and together for the grace of unity in one house of prayer. This fact of a simultaneous prayer directed toward *one* goal was in itself such an immense spiritual reality, brought about by the development of the ecumenical movement, that a way simply had to be found in which all could really walk together. The formula proposed by Paul Couturier could be accepted by everyone: To pray for the grace of unity as God wants it and in the way He wants it.

This was not "a clever Catholic move," an indirect means of gaining some kind of influence over "the others"; it was the honest expression of the fact that our faith and our hope are rooted in God, and an expression also of the conviction that both our disunity and our unity are a mystery which God alone knows in all its intricacies, and which transcends everything *we* believe we have done to clarify it. Thus, this prayer was not the expression of a "little faith" but, on the contrary, of a faith big enough to allow us to put all our security and our hopes in God.

Today, the World Unity Octave is being celebrated every January in a great many places. Every year since 1936 I have preached during this week in French cities and those of adjoining countries. I can bear witness to the openmindedness of my listeners, who have increased in numbers over the years. And especially can I attest to the deep and deeply moving interest which grips those who attend these observances. It is indeed a week of grace that is given to us every year. Many a pastor has remarked that his parish has changed because of it. We can assure those who are willing to commit themselves in the fullness of faith, in hope and in purity of heart, to this work, that the Lord will be with them, because in this work we are directly, in a literal sense, doing His will.

Cooperation in Intellectual and Scientific Pursuits

This kind of cooperation can be put into action by those who have a vocation to teach, by parents and teachers in all varieties of schools wherever there is a problem of genuine truth in literature, in history, in topics such as the Oriental Schism, the Reformation, religious wars. Generally speaking, everything that reflects truthfulness to facts and genuine Christian behavior also works for reunion and has an ecumenical value. There are specialists needed in ecumenical work: people who have the time, the resources, the vocation and the grace, perhaps even the official mandate to research the difficult questions of theology and history which grow out of ecumenical dialogue. Here as everywhere it is true that everyone must do his duty in the place where he is put. "God," says Paul, "is not a God of disorder, but of peace" (1 Cor. 14: 33, 40).

But it is one thing to write an expert paper on questions of ecumenical interest, and another thing to act in a way that has ecumenical value. Every Christian act can and should be of value ecumenically; that is to say, it can advance the unity of the sons and daughters of God in Jesus Christ. Every time we judge a point in history or in Christian dogma with greater accuracy; every time we form in ourselves or project a concept of God, of the Gospel, of the Church, that is closer to the truth than the one we held before; every time we participate more deeply in the sacraments; every time we succeed in better comprehending a piece of art or the meaning of style in church architecture; every time we prepare more conscientiously a certain text (whether it is something scholarly or something as simple as an announcement of church services, a leaflet, or a pamphlet); every time we find the true words that make our prayer one of greater sincerity—every time that we do any of these things, we do something that is of real ecumenical value.

The sphere of ecumenical action is in reality immeasurable; it extends to the entire life of the Church. And it is obvious that everyone can and should do his or her part, if not specifically as a specialist, at least as a participant in an action in which the entire Church is engaged.

Everyone is a participant—a combatant, as it were—and in more ways than one. In the present development of historical consciousness, the term "collective responsibility" or, what is pretty much the same, historical responsibility, has come to the fore. Let us leave aside at this point the technical discussion of the exact limits of such responsibility, and for practical reasons let us concentrate instead on the reality to which this responsibility represents a response. Just as creation is not only an act of the past situated somewhere "in the beginning," but rather a first impetus being continued in the total historical development of the universe, so also are the great Christian schisms not only events that happened *once* on a precisely determinable date; they occur every day in history—the history in which we live for a moment, or rather in which for a brief span of time we are all co-actors, though in various degrees. The Oriental Schism, the dissension of the Reformation—all this is still taking place. But these immense historical facts cannot be separated from certain historical realities. The Reformation was not accomplished within the framework of the Church of St. Augustine or St. Gregory the Great, but within the framework of the Church of the sixteenth century, characterized as it was by all we mean when we speak of the Western Middle Ages with their scholasticism, the papacy, the secular organization of Christendom, the pilgrimages and indulgences. However, it is possible to imagine a state of affairs in the Church which would *not* have produced the Reformation, a situation which would *not* have made possible the terrible division. Rudolph von Harnack wrote about the decree on justification issued by the Council of Trent in the year 1547, eleven months after the death of Luther: "It is doubtful that the Reformation would have developed if this decree had been issued by the Lateran Council at the beginning of the century and had been absorbed into the body and blood of the Church" (*History of Dogmas* III, 711).

My point is this: Every time we act in such a way that the split between East and West or the schism of the Reformation would, in human or historical terms, again be inevitable, we become co-responsible for it. By the same token, every time we behave in such a way that, had this behavior been the case centuries ago, the evil of the division between the East and West or the tragedy of the dissensions of the Reformation could have been avoided, we are doing our part in the healing of these evils. This holds true for Catholics as well as for our separated brothers.

"Woe to him through whom scandals come!"

"Blessed be the peace makers!"

Again you will say: I am a layman. What can I do?

The scope of responsibility is subject to change. Our responsibility increases in proportion to the greater knowledge that we gain. Therefore we can distinguish two main groups:

1. Those laymen who are not specifically called in this respect.

2. Those laymen who, because of their specialized knowledge, have a special responsibility.

Laymen in the first group can always participate in the movement by keeping informed, by subscribing, perhaps, to a publication in this field, just as subscribing to a mission magazine is an effective means of sustaining our interest in the missions. In addition, such people should do their utmost in living up to what has been suggested above as to personal attitude and prayer. They can ask their clergy to speak on this subject, maybe arrange something for the parish or some parish organizations on the occasion of the

Unity Octave in January. Everyone can do his part to help develop a *well-informed* public opinion within the Church.

Although the faithful neither participate in the making of decisions in this matter nor exercise any governing functions, they can and even should make their wishes known in a reasonable and intelligible manner. History has recorded more than one occasion where decisions or initiatives of great importance were taken in response to requests or urgings from laymen. There is Catherine of Siena who brings about the return of the pope from Avignon to Rome; there is a group of students which succeeds in having Abbé Lacordaire appointed preacher at the Cathedral of Notre Dame, to name but two examples. Of course, it all depends on the way in which things are approached. A demanding or lecturing tone has never been appreciated by the Church. "Common sense" is only a modest name for the Christian virtue of prudence. But prudence does not mean timidity or passivity, even less comfortable or lazy indifference.

Laymen in the second group, those who have more possibilities and therefore a greater moral responsibility, could again be divided into two categories, although the criteria for both can often be found combined in one person.

A person may possess a certain specialized, perhaps scientific knowledge. To begin with, it does not matter in which field, for as I said before, every serious work contributes to the creation of an atmosphere of credibility in which tensions relax, and every such atmosphere has an ecumenical value by and of itself. When a Catholic mathematician or geographer is thoroughly versed in his subject and, in addition, is a decent man in his heart, his qualities will make it possible that Catholics as a whole will appear to other men, be they Christian or not, as acceptable and worthy of trust. But there are special fields where reliable work as such can have great and immediate ecumenical possibilities: the field of philosophy, and especially history.

Philosophy is important here because it is capable of developing an attitude of openmindedness and dialogue, and it can clarify within its sphere certain basic fundamentals for ecumenical action.

This is equally true for history, for various reasons. First of all, because it is of absolutely decisive importance how on the one side, the papacy and the Middle Ages are presented, and how, on the other side, the Reformation, the personality of the reformers, their intentions, and their actual work are studied. In Germany, Luther remains the giant personality still occupying such a place of prominence, even in the purely national domain, that an unjust or deprecatory evaluation of him could erect an insurmountable obstacle for every rapprochement.[3]

Another reason for the importance of history is this: the *historical* assessment of the facts and of the texts wherein our differences are manifested is an indispensable prerequisite for a healthy and effective beginning in ecumen-

---

3. Except for the indeed too unrealistic last sentence, I would like to quote here this passage by Ernest Juenger: "Traces of Luther remain indelibly in our fate. He enters into all our great decisions. Any rebirth will be of no avail, not so much because of his doctrines and his reforms but because of the symbolic strength of his personality—the symbol of his spirit—unless there should be a pope in the future who would muster the authority to canonize him and to elevate him into the ranks of the Fathers of the Church" (*Jahre der Okkupation*, 1947, p. 289).

ical activity. Therefore, anything that can be established as historically accurate in those points which directly or indirectly touch on the preparation, the beginning, and the development of the great Christian schisms, is at the same time a strengthening of the foundation for ecumenical work. Tons of good concrete will yet have to be poured into this foundation for some time to come, as into the foundation of a building that is to be erected on uneven ground. The same is true in even greater measure of every reliable work in the field of exegesis or patristics, that is to say, studies of the work of those great Christian figures who laid the foundations of theology between the second century and the sixth.

Certain of the faithful have an *ecumenical vocation* in the essential or at least in the broad meaning of the word. By that I mean a call to do something specific in the service of Christian unity: To become a member, for example, of a group which devotes itself to personal encounters or to work which has the purpose of furthering the ecumenical idea; or to start such a group in one's own city or parish (of course in agreement and cooperation with a priest); or to stimulate interest for the Unity Octave. Having travelled every January for twenty-five years through France and sometimes the adjoining countries, I know that the Unity Octave flourishes most in those places where there is someone who takes care of it, who devotes himself to it. Very often this is a layman or laywoman.

How does one know whether or not he has an ecumenical vocation? What is it like?

A vocation comes into being from the encounter with a certain task and being attracted to it; through the existence of the necessary means for carrying out this task; through opportunities and, finally, through the fact that the work planned finds recognition on the part of the responsible leaders of the Christian community, on the level of that community. If we find ourselves confronted by an urgent human or Christian task, if a work useful for the kingdom of God comes our way, a work which will not be done by anyone unless we take it on, then we are, as it were, called —and we are under an obligation. A responsibility has been placed on us, and therefore, in the broad meaning of the word, we have been enjoined with a mission. Nonetheless, the call we have heard and the attraction we have felt must, so to speak, be reinforced by the presence of the required talents or the necessary resources. This might involve for example understanding—not necessarily in the form of specific knowledge but certainly in the form of good common sense—balance of personality, intellectual calmness, and at least a silent approbation by those who are responsible for the life and order of the Church.

The active participation in meetings, work-circles with non-Catholics, in short what is called the Una Sancta work, is subject to a regulation which is specifically explained in the encyclical *Ecclesia Catholica* of December, 1949. This document recalls what for Catholics is a matter of course, that every aspect of interdenominational relations belongs properly within the domain of episcopal supervision. The permission of the appropriate bishop is therefore required if an activity of purely local participation is involved, or the approbation of the Holy See in the case of a work of national or international scope. Laymen are free to associate with non-Catholics. As for friendships or other personal relations, no other obligations apply but those guiding all personal Christian activity. If an organized, formal type of meeting is involved, however, with the purpose of denominational confrontation, the bishop or the vicar general of the diocese must be consulted, or an authorized priest. If theological discussions with Protestants are intended, formal permission is required, and the bishop must be kept informed of the proceedings.

The document cited above states that no special permission is required for joint activities of Catholics and non-Catholics in the area of natural rights or for the defense of Christian principles in the life of society. One merely remains subject to the general rules of loyal Catholicity: prudence and knowledge of the subject matter, possibly supplemented by appropriate advice. In this area belong for example: the fight against pornography, alcoholism, poverty, race hatred, use of atomic weapons, war, atheistic communism, or actions for the protection of youth, the protection of animals, help for displaced persons, membership in the Red Cross, the participation in communal political groups, and so on. This is a broad area where, as we have seen, separated Christians can get to know each other, even to appreciate one another for their Christianity, and thus pave the way to approaches of an expressly religious nature.

What Can We Hope For?

For everything, where the Holy Spirit is at work. "Jesus," said Charles de Foucauld, "is the Lord of the impossible." If God has indeed begun something in the direction of the reunion of Christians, who can put limits to His work?

There is only one thing for us to do: with all our strength to believe and to cooperate with the power of His grace. He knows the end, the goal. If anyone would dare to attempt a human prognosis, he must immediately realize this: Humanly speaking, reunion is impossible. But since so much has become a reality, there is justification for the hope that even more may be accomplished.

Indeed, reunion seems impossible as long as one looks realistically at the absolute character of certain contradictory beliefs. All the more so because no one is permitted in conscience to make *concessions* in matters of what to him appear to be the truth. Thus, one side holds fast, for example, to the dogma of papal infallibility, the other side (the Orthodox) to the belief that the infallibility of the Church is vested exclusively in the Councils, while the evangelical Christians cannot admit any kind of infallibility for any ecclesiastic office in the Church. And if one thinks of the centuries of separate development which cannot simply be put aside in a day, not even in several generations, if one thinks of the many practical questions, even though they appear to be only of secondary importance (e.g., for the Eastern Church the laws regarding the indissolubility of marriage), if one contemplates the fact that as soon as the hoped-for union was achieved, a mere trifle could suffice to fan again the old antitheses whose testimonies and texts are after all indelibly etched into history —then, humanly speaking, it appears evident that reunion is impossible.

And yet, many a way has already been opened. Things which thirty or forty years ago seemed impossible are facts today. Even in matters of doctrine, we have come to see—and without concession to a mistaken liberalism—

that points which have been greatly disputed or which seemed to be decisive points of contrast, must not necessarily be devisive issues, if only they are well explained. Take, for example, the "issue" of the Holy Spirit (filioque) between the Eastern and Western Church, the question of justification between the Protestants and us: these two points were absolutely decisive in the beginning of the schisms. Better defined, they leave a way open for mutual understanding. For other questions explanations are undoubtedly possible and will be found or worked out. Already, advances in other areas are in the making—in Scripture and tradition, faith and the sacraments. Comparative Bible studies have been gaining more and more ground in recent years. Other important agreements, as for instance in the area of prayer forms, could be pointed to.

But let us not indulge in rash predictions of the future. Let us labor! Let us pay the price for such a great undertaking—the price of toil, prayer, suffering, but also the price of patience and perseverance of which St. Paul speaks in a manner that surprises us because we do not expect these qualities to produce what he says they will, namely, hope. "Hope does not disappoint," he says "because the charity of God is poured forth in our hearts by the Holy Spirit who has been given to us" (Rom. 5: 4-5).

9

EMMANUEL MARIA
HEUFELDER, OSB

THE COUNCIL
AND
REUNION

RARELY HAS AN event of recent history so affected the whole of Christendom as the announcement of an ecumenical council by Pope John XXIII. The exaggerated expectations which came to the fore in the immediate wake of the pope's announcement had of course to give way to the more sober reflection that the time for a council of union had not yet come. But Pope John emphasized repeatedly that he did not look to the council as to a mere inter-ecclesiastical affair but considered it with a view to all of Christianity. And he made this unmistakably clear when in his Apostolic Letter of Pentecost, 1960, he created, in addition to the preparatory commissions, a separate Secretariat for Christian Unity with these words: "So that we may further demonstrate our love and our good will towards those who are marked by the name Christians, even though they are separated from the Apostolic See, and to enable them to follow the work of the Council and thus more easily find the road to that union for which Jesus Christ implored his heavenly Father with such ardent prayer, we institute a special secretariat which will be under the chairmanship of a cardinal to be appointed by us, and which will be organized in accordance with the directions issued for the commissions."

Soon afterwards Cardinal Bea was entrusted with the direction of this secretariat.

Not only was the creation of such a secretariat for the purpose of establishing contacts with the non-Catholic Christians an historic event, signaling a new beginning in the relationships between the Roman Catholic Church and the "separated brethren," the words which the pope used in this context are of decisive importance. He spoke of "those adorned with the name Christians" ("qui Christiano nomine decorantur"), and he pointed to the profound union which exists through Baptism (Rom. 6: 3-5) between all who are embraced by the saving grace of Christ. With obvious deliberation he evoked "that union for which Jesus Christ implored his heavenly Father with such ardent prayers" (John 17). In the longing for this union desired by Christ Himself, all who call themselves Christians must unite.

Although it is part of the self-appraisal of the Catholic Church, as well as Catholic belief, that the Roman Church possesses within itself all that is necessary for the unity intended by Christ, the pope knows as well as any Christian that Christ's Church has a divine and a human side, and that the human frailty and sinfulness of its members time and again obscures its divine essence. It is precisely for this reason that the pope called the responsible shepherds together for a council in order to initiate a renewal of the Church from within and thereby eliminate the obstacles which on our side stand in the way of a united Christianity.

The Council, therefore, must become a *reform council*. We know how in the centuries that preceded the breakup of the unity of the Church during the Reformation, the call for a "reform of the head and the members" was sounded ever more loudly. Because this call was not heeded in time, the Christian community broke apart. Now, through the council, the call for reform is sounding again, in order to help restore the broken unity.

It is worthy of note what other Christians who are sincerely concerned with the schism thought of the action of the pope, and what they told their co-religionists about it. Here is a quote: "The assertion that this council is an exclusively Roman Catholic affair which does not concern us Evangelical Christians is, knowingly or unknowingly, misleading because John XXIII clearly indicated that this Council is intended to be one of clarification and timely renewal of the Roman Catholic Church in order to make it easier for other Christian confessions to find union with Rome. Is such a renewal of the Roman Church of no concern to us? It is a pioneering step on the part of the Roman Church on the way to the future, even if union is not possible at this time."

If Protestants take the Council so seriously, would it not be for Catholics a "sin against the Holy Spirit" to take any less seriously the call for renewal which comes from the council to us?

What Is Involved in This Reform?

To gain the right concept of what is now taking place, we have to remember that ever since the beginning of this century we have been involved in a renewal movement decisively initiated and carried on by the great popes of this period.

Pope Leo XIII began this work of renewal. When at the beginning of this century he consecrated it to the Sacred Heart of the Redeemer, it was more than a subjective act of the pope's personal piety. The pope wanted to lead the world to the heart of the divine revelation. He wanted to open to the world anew the mystery that "God is love" (1 John 4: 8). He wanted to awaken the resources of the heart, the forces of Christian charity, in the face of the destructive moral diseases of the time, egotism and individualism, intellectualism and rationalism. Christianity was to be shown what in the providential plan is the only effective answer to the demands of Marxist socialism and the oncoming threats embodied in collectivism and Bolshevism: the realization of a truly Christian community. Only in this perspective do the social encyclicals of Leo XIII take on their full meaning.

The holy pope Pius X then expressed the call to reform clearly in his motto, "the restoration of all things in Christ," which implied a broad, far-reaching regeneration. He pointed with great emphasis to the source of all regeneration: Christ, the incarnate Son of God who in the mystery of the Eucharist continuously makes present His work of redemption, building through the mystery of this sacrament his own Mystical Body. With liturgical renewal and the "active participation" of the faithful in the celebration of the Eucharist, the foundation was simultaneously laid for the "active participation of the faithful in the hierarchical apostolate" to which Pius XI later called the laity of the Church in his proclamation of "Catholic Action."

In the process of overcoming Modernism, Pius X again directed attention to the essentially supernatural character of Christian revelation, and thereby opened the doors to a profound renewal of theological thinking and the ascetic life.

While the supernatural foundations of the Church were thus being reaffirmed, the Church could turn anew to its mission in and for the world. With Benedict XV, the great preacher of peace, the Church moved once more among the nations. Through the far-reaching charitable activities of this pope, the Roman Church proved herself again "first in the solidarity of love."

Pope Benedict clearly saw the epoch of revolutionary changes which entered history with the First World War. He was probably the first to use the phrase of a "new age," when in September, 1914, in a conversation with the then Benedictine Abbot Primate, Fidelis von Stotzingen, he compared our epoch with that of the migration of the nations; he explained he had purposely chosen St. Benedict's name in order to orientate this new age toward God, as St. Benedict had done on the threshold of the Middle Ages. Pope Benedict realized the importance of the East for the developments that were to come. He founded the Oriental Institute in Rome as a base for the study of the Eastern Church and as a point of contact with the Orthodox. While he thus attempted to build a bridge to the separated Churches of the East, he pointed at the same time to the only possible way for the reunion of divided Christendom: "Not that they become Latin, only that they become Catholic, is necessary," he said. Pope Pius XI later expanded this orientation towards the East by founding the Russicum and by appealing to the various religious orders to devote themselves to work with the Eastern Churches.

With the consecration of the first Chinese bishop, Benedict XV also initiated a new direction in the missionary activities of the Church which has been effectively affirmed by his successors. A great number of missionary territories have already been entrusted to native clergy.

"The Church is awakening in souls," it was said in the pontificate of Pius XI. And his proclamation of Catholic Action ushered in a new appreciation of the status and the duties of the laity.

Pius XII's encyclical on the Mystical Body of Christ gave both expression and recognition to this newly awakened Church-consciousness. The same pope also cleared the way for the continuation of the ideas of Pope Pius X by means of far-reaching liturgical reform, and he had words of direction for all areas of human life and introduced measures intended to facilitate the process of renewal.

Thus, the Church was interiorly fortified by the Holy Spirit so that "the gates of Hell should not prevail against her" when the great anti-Christian movements of Bolshevism and National Socialism took on ever more threatening proportions. Stronger than ever before, the papacy stood as a rock during the years of the Second World War and the post-war period. Pius XII distinctly recognized the development of history toward "one world," as we witness it today, and in his addresses and encyclicals he contributed building stones for a future world order based on a Christian foundation.

At the same time, while the renewal within the Catholic Church was progressing, the work of the Holy Spirit began to be noticeable also among the separated Christians. Just as in the Catholic Bible movement the Word of God was brought closer to us again in its meaning and influence on our lives, so Protestantism had its reawakening of interest in the sacramental life, and in both cases there began a liturgical renewal. Of this area it can also be said: "The Church is awakening in souls." People are seriously concerned with a deeper understanding of the essence of the Church and of the mission of the Church in the world. The ecumenical movement is a visible expression of the fact that the longing for the "One, Holy, Catholic, and Apostolic Church" is growing everywhere. Pius XII, John XXIII, and Paul VI have openly acknowledged the working of the Holy Spirit which is evident in these movements.

In the Eastern Church, too, the desire for union has come alive with hope. Under Communist oppression, the Church of the East has produced such a great number of martyrs and confessors that we expect especially from her a new fruitfulness in the time to come.

Thus, everywhere forces can be seen at work pushing toward a renewal. Against the grave and dark background of present-day history, a Pentecostal storm seems again to be in the making in the kingdom of God on earth, destined to shake from the tree of the Church all that is dead, in preparation for a new springtime. In one of his last addresses to Catholic youth, Pius XII spoke specifically of just such an imminent spring.

Looking at it from this point of view, the announcement of a council of reform by Pope John XXIII appears as a climactic act intended to fuse all the earlier beginnings of renewal into one. In his most important utterance on the council, the pope wrote on April 24, 1959, to the clergy of Venice that he had announced the council "in obedience to an inspiration whose immediacy we felt like a sudden, unexpected touch." In the letter of Pentecost Sunday, 1960, in which he appointed the preparatory commission for the council, he again pointed out specifically that the idea to convoke a council had come to him "Superno Dei nutu"—through God's exalted inspiration. Thus, the immediate call of the Holy Spirit becomes visible in the announcement of the council. "Let us plead and hope," the pope's letter to the clergy of Venice continues, "that the council will repeat the spectacle of the Apostles gathered in Jerusalem after the ascension of our Lord: the union of hearts in thought and prayer gathered with Peter and around Peter, with the shepherds, the lambs, and the sheep." The pope clearly was thinking of the first Pentecost, of the Holy Spirit as the soul of the Mystical Body of Christ. From Him he expected, as he wrote, "the energies that make us capable of new deeds."

Pope John believed that the Holy Spirit even today can "renew the face of the earth," that He can bring about even today what is described in the Acts of the Apostles in the words: "all were of one mind and one soul." With that idea in mind, the pope issued this prayer intention for the month after Pentecost in 1960: "That the faithful may ardently implore the help of the Holy Spirit for the restoration of the union of all Christians in the one true faith and the one Church."

Only thus can we comprehend all that is meant by the simple words in which Pope John described the goal of the council: "The main goal of the Council will be to further an increase of the Catholic faith and a salutory renewal of morality among the Christian people, and to adopt the discipline of the Church to the necessities of our time."

The "increase of the Catholic faith" does not depend on any new dogma, not even on the continuation of the dogmatic deliberations of the First Vatican Council, but on whether or not we rediscover the elemental truth of the operation of the Holy Spirit in the Church. This reality of the Holy Spirit who introduces us into all truth, who recalls to our mind all that the Lord has said, who will convince the world that there is sin and that there is a judgment (John 14: 26; 16: 8-11)—has this reality not all too thoroughly vanished from our consciousness? Do we not perhaps expect the renewal of the Church and of the world all too much from our modern methods and new human activities, necessary as they may be as an expression of our readiness to cooperate with grace?

All the promises of our Redeemer before His return to the Father culminate in the promise of the sending of the Holy Spirit, the "other paraclete," "another to befriend you," as Msgr. Knox so beautifully renders this phrase; who will remain with us to bring the work of Christ to its completion (John 14: 16).

Anyone who is charged with the care of souls time and again experiences the crushing impotence of all pastoral efforts, confronted as he is by the spirit of the time which secularizes man more and more, and by the demonic forces which become evermore evident.

In this situation, the only thing that can really help is a renewed faith in the Holy Spirit who alone has the power to awaken life even where, humanly speaking, everything seems dead, as the powerful vision of the prophet Ezechiel portrays it in chapter 37 of his prophecies.

In this Holy Spirit we must believe again with a faith that moves mountains. For the coming of this Spirit we must pray, full of faith, as the disciples did before the first Pentecost. Again and again Pope John called us to this kind of prayer full of faith. On this prayer, he said, depends the success of the council, more than on all human endeavors.

Of course, whether or not our belief in the Holy Spirit is genuine and our prayer for his coming sincere shows in our readiness to undergo the "metanoia," the conversion, for which Peter, the first pope, had called in his Pentecost sermon; it shows in our willingness to reform ourselves—the moral renewal for which Pope John was hoping.

But here, too, what counts in the first place are not a few isolated reform measures; what matters is the fundamental, total attitude a Christian must have so that the one thing which determines Christian life can unfold—just as what counts in the matter of faith are not some *particular* truths, but *the* fundamental truth of the reality of the Holy Spirit, sent to us to "teach [us] *all* the truth" (John 16: 13).

Wherein, then, does the deepest meaning, the essential and fundamental content of the Christian revelation lie? (If we disunited Christians are to find each other again, it is imperative that we recognize the ultimate foundations of the revelation which we have in common.)

The divine reality which unfolds before our eyes through revelation, and finally in the incarnation of the Son of God, is not exhausted by any one doctrine, by any single truth about God: "I came that they may have life, and have it more abundantly" (John 10: 10).

This revelation is *life*. That is why our Lord specifically says that only he who lives it can recognize this truth: "My teaching is not my own, but his who sent me. If anyone desires to do his will, he will know of the teaching whether it is from God, or whether I speak on my own authority (John 7: 17).

But what is the "life" to which revelation gives us access? What does it consist of? What is the real core and substance of divine revelation? Certainly this: that "God is love" (1 John 4: 8), and that He wants to enter with men into a communion of love, taking them into Himself, into His own triune life, the union of the Father and the Son in the Spirit of love.

This love of the God who reveals Himself flows not only to the individual man, it also unites all those who are embraced by this love: "That they may be one, even as we are one" (John 17: 22).

This unity of the disciples of Christ among each other is the visible sign that they have indeed accepted the message of Christ: "By this will all men know that you are my disciples, if you have love for one another" (John 13: 35).

This mutual charity is, so to speak, what in a sacrament is called "the visible sign" by which the invisible grace, the love of God, is made manifest and imparted. It is for this reason that love of God and love of neighbor cannot be separated. And therefore St. John can say: "He who does not love, does not know God; for God is love" (1 John 48: 8).

Therefore St. Paul can proclaim that even a faith so great that it can move mountains is nothing if love is not a part of it (1 Cor. 13: 2).

Therefore, the separation of faith and charity both in theory and practice, which is so frequent among us Christians, amounts to "heresy" and "schism," to an arbitrary selection from the Christian substance, to "separation." All those who separate faith and charity in the practice of

life are heretics and schismatics, irrespective of the confession to which they belong.

For precisely this reason, Pope John hoped and wished
that his council would become a "spectacle of truth, union,
and love" ("spectacle" certainly not in the sense of dis-
play, but in the meaning of making visible the union of
truth and charity in the Catholic Church).

The Church has thus to manifest itself before the world
so that anyone who is of good will can see that here is the
totality of the truth of Christ, but here also is genuine love
and therefore unity. The claim of the Catholic Church to
possess revealed truth in its fullness will cease to be an
offense and a stumbling block if it becomes plain that we
take the commandment of love as seriously as Christ intended it to be taken; therein we will find the power to
unite the disciples of Christ.

Unless unity and charity are joined to truth, truth cannot have any effect in the world: "I pray . . . that all may
be one, even as thou, Father, in me and I in thee; that
they also may be one in us, that the world may believe that
thou hast sent me. And the glory that thou hast given me,
I have given to them, that they may be one, even as we are
one: I in them and thou in me; that they may be perfected
in unity . . ." (John 17: 21-23).

This joining together of truth and love cannot possibly
be a threat to the truth.

If, as we have seen, the innermost substance of revelation is the fact that "the charity of God is poured forth
in our hearts by the Holy Spirit who has been given to us"
(Rom. 5: 5), then charity and truth simply cannot and
must not be allowed to be separated. Then it is also obvi-

ous that Christian truth cannot be perceived in its fullness by the intellect alone.

The truth of Christ is, after all, not merely a set of ideas that must be believed; it is a person: "I am . . . the truth," says the Lord (John 14: 6).

The truth of Christ, therefore, can only be accepted by one who is willing to enter into a personal relationship with Christ by opening himself to His love with all the consequences that will spring from this commitment. That is why the Lord combines with the concept of truth two other concepts: "I am the way, the truth, and the life." By this he says that we can accept and possess Him as the embodiment of truth only if we totally, without reservation, make a decision for Him. Whoever does not take this into consideration, is in danger of slighting Christian truth, or does not see it as it is.

And there is something else that is rooted in the singular nature of the revelation of Christian truth. There can be only *one* truth regarding God and the Christ who is the Truth; yet such is the fullness of this truth that no man can comprehend and exhaust all of its riches. Consequently, this one truth can be seen and expressed by different people in different ways. It can be beheld from varied points of view just as a stretch of scenery, a range of mountains through which we wander, offers different views to our eyes as we progress through it. This may be one reason why the Lord has handed down to us not just one Gospel but four—four which at first glance do not always agree on every point. God ordained that the concept of Christ as we receive it from the Synoptic Gospels is contrasted by a very different view in the Gospel of

John. It would be an arbitrary choice, even heresy, if some-one were to admit as valid only *one* Gospel, only one view. Therefore, since the earliest Christian times there have come into existence various theological "schools," all of which are attempting in various ways to penetrate and to develop the truths that have been revealed to us. We have the theology of the Eastern Church, we have Augustine and Thomas, Bonaventure and Duns Scotus, to name but a few.

The Church has given preference to some of these schools which she thought presented the truth revealed to us somewhat better than others or with greater safeguards against errors. But no one theological school can ever claim absolute validity for itself.

Nevertheless, human frailty being what it is, such claims have been made, time and again, and the result always was a narrowing—the opposite of catholicity. Among the Apostles we already find the "dispute for precedence" (and this part of the "apostolic tradition" has, sad to say, been most faithfully preserved in all Christian denomina-tions); and still in apostolic times, we see the serious ten-sions resulting from the controversy between the Chris-tian converts from Judaism and the Christian converts from paganism.

Such a tendency toward narrowness and a misconcep-tion of divine revelation, born of human frailty and sinful-ness, was the reason why the people of Israel did not attain salvation even though, as Paul affirms, they have ". . . the covenants and the legislation and the worship and the promises" (Rom. 9: 4-5). The Israel of old confused the time-conditioned form in which revelation was brought to the Chosen People, with its substance. To divine revelation, which had come to them through Moses and the prophets, they added human ordinances and endowed these with the same or even higher value than the commands of revelation.

This danger, the narrowing of divine revelation by man, can be avoided only by our willingness to love; yet this narrowing runs through the entire history of the kingdom of God on earth, and affects the history of the Church. It is in fact one of the main reasons for the divisions of the disciples of Jesus. There is only *one* Church of Jesus Christ. There can be only one Church just as there is only one Christ. But faced with the diversity of mankind, of nations and of times, the Church of Jesus Christ can, in the course of history, take on various forms while the fundamental structure which it received from Christ may be fully preserved. In complete fidelity to the substance of Christ's legacy (and precisely because it is the legacy of the unfathomable riches of Christ), the Church, over and over again, can show and unfold new aspects of the "kingdom" which He wants to build among us.

Christianity found its first expression in the soil of the Greco-Roman culture; this fact determined to a great degree the form in which the Church developed. Thus, the Christian message came to the people of the West in a Roman-Latin framework. This was significant for the Germanic peoples who, in addition to their Christianization, were also in need of cultural formation. But, however precious the Roman-Latin form may be, it is not the only one that is valid. Standing beside it with equal right is the Eastern form of Christian and churchly life. Time and again, the popes have emphasized this fact, and we have to thank them for it.

Who would dare to set limits to the Holy Spirit, as though all possible forms of the realization of Christian life were already exhausted! Once the nations of Africa and Asia have become Christian, might it not be possible that under the impetus of the Holy Spirit new ways of theological thinking and new forms of Christian living will develop which might present the fullness of revelation even more lucidly than it has been done thus far? At the Church's first Pentecost, the people said in amazement: ". . . how have we heard each his own language" (Acts 2:8). And of the heavenly Jerusalem, the Seer of the Apocalypse says: "And the city has no need of the sun or the moon. . . . the glory of God lights it up, and the Lamb is the lamp thereof. And the nations shall walk by the light thereof; and the kings of the earth shall bring their glory and honor into it. . . . And they shall bring the glory and honor of nations into it" (Apoc. 21: 23-24, 26).

Every missionary "colonialism" is thus rejected not only as it pertains to the persons whose mission it is to preach the glad tidings of Christ, but also as it concerns the form in which the Gospel of Christ can be preached and accepted. Not only have the nations a right to their own native clergy, they also have the right to expect that their own characteristics may be given room and the chance to develop an individual form of Christian life in somewhat the same way as it was formerly possible for the nations of the Greco-Roman civilization.

With that we have arrived at the third point Pope John had in mind as a goal for the council: To adapt the discipline of the Church to the necessities of our time. There are various ways in which the Christian idea can be lived, depending on the character of individuals and nations, and depending also on the level of development through which mankind as a whole is passing at a given period of time.

This history of the religious orders is proof that Christian perfection, which clearly consists in perfect love of God and neighbor, can be striven for in many different ways. Who would not admit that there are also quite imperfect forms—even distortions—of the intended ideal, so that time and again reform is necessary?

In the natural sphere, there are various ways in which parents exercise their God-given authority within the family. So also can the judicial power, which Christ undoubtedly gave to His Church, be exercised with more or less perfection by the individual bearers of this God-given authority. Therefore, an examination of the Church's laws is a good thing, and we ought to be grateful to Pope John that such a probing look was included in the announcement of the council.

A point which is of special importance with regard to the efforts for a reunion of divided Christendom is the primacy of the pope. One will have to admit—even while insisting in principle on the recognition of the Petrine office—that the manner in which this office is carried out permits variation in forms; that besides the strict centralized forms which, for the good of the Church, have developed in the West (in conflict with various state religions and the infringements of secular power on the life of the Church), there also exists the possibility of a more federalized form which seems better suited to the East.

For all these reasons, reform is necessary in the Church again and again, as well as an examination of conscience as to whether we as members and organs of the Church of

Jesus Christ do indeed accept and transmit divine revelation in the proper way; or whether we perhaps merely
equate time-honored customs and habits with the substance of the Christian faith; or whether, through human
concepts of the Church and its life, we actually obscure
the light of revealed truth.

We must ask ourselves over and over: Do we distinguish sufficiently between the totality of revealed truth,
which is one, and the human vessels and organs to which
this truth is entrusted? In humility and contrition we must
admit and remind ourselves that through our imperfec-
tion and sinfulness we have all too often hindered the
work of God.

Therefore we ought to be grateful to the Lord that He
has taken the "reform of the head and the members" which
is so necessary for His Church, into His own hands; that
for some time already, through the great popes He sent
the Church, He had begun a renewal of the head; that
through Pope John XXIII He not only announced a council intended to promote an "increase in the Catholic faith
and a salutary renewal of morality among the Christian
people, and the adaptation of Church discipline to the
necessities of the time," but that He showed impressively
in the person of that pope what it is that matters first of
all in this reform.

Friedrich Heer wrote in an article on the coronation of
Pope John XXIII in November, 1958: "The most important
business in the Catholic Church today is the rebirth of
authority through the warm, strong, bold, personal spirit
of a pontifex who is governor, shepherd, and father, all in
one. If the many millions of statistically counted Catholics
are to become personally mature human beings, fully

Christian and fully human, then—humanly speaking—this can only come about through the rebirth of the father in the Church."

Then Heer speaks of the reunion of divided Christendom, especially in relation to the Eastern Church, as one of the most urgent tasks, and continues: "Whoever had any close and personal contact with people of the East, especially the Eastern Church, knows that the price for the reunion of the Churches, the Eastern and the Roman Catholic Church, is considerably higher than we imagine. It requires on the part of the West a willingness to trust, an appreciation of brotherliness and openness, an unreservedness which we hardly dare to imagine."

After all that happened, however, under the pontificate of Pope John, it is possible to say: the rebirth of the father in the Church has begun. Pope John possessed this "willingness to trust, this appreciation of brotherliness, openness, and unreservedness." He was like the disciple of the Lord whose name he had taken and whose deepest concern was Pope John's own concern: "Children, love one another!"

In this spirit of kindliness and openness, the pope came to use an entirely new language in his contact with the separated Christians whom he called "brothers," and he specifically asked their prayers for the success of the council.

Dostoevski lets the monk Zossima say: "Before many a thought one hesitates, stopped by doubt, especially in seeing the sins of men, and one asks himself: Shall it be done by force or with humble love? Always decide in favor of humble love! Once you have resolved to follow that course, you will overcome the world. Humble love

is an awesome power; it is the greatest force of all, and
there is nothing like it."

All reforms begin in the hearts of men, with a renewal
of their interior dispositions. Only from these dispositions
does right action follow. The biblical call for metanoia,
change of heart, also received a new impetus through the
example of Pope John. He himself began the new reform in
the spirit of humble love with which he was filled.

But the reform of the "head" is not enough. The spirit
of humble charity must permeate all the members and
organs of the Church: bishops and priests, clergy and
laity, the men in the world and those in monasteries, the
spiritual authorities and offices, the Church's organizations and associations.

For this, of course, the coming of a new pentecostal
spirit is needed. Pope John specifically and repeatedly
stated his belief in a new pentecostal miracle, and he
called on Christendom to pray for him for such a new
pentecostal spirit, just as once the first disciples did, gathered around Peter. But we must also be willing to be committed by this spirit of Pentecost. We must not flee before
the storm behind the walls erected by our egotism, our
self-contentment and self-sufficiency, seeking refuge in
our petty, narrow conceits and prejudices.

Above all, we must overcome the fear of what humble
love may require of us. It demands that we take literally
and accept seriously what our Lord told us in the Sermon
on the Mount about our relations with other men: "To
him who asks of thee, give . . ." (Mat. 5: 42). Humble
charity demands that we be prepared to walk the path
of humility and renunciation which our Lord has shown
us: "Have this mind in you which was also in Christ
Jesus . . ." (Phil. 2: 5-8). Charity demands our readiness

for that surrender of our own ego of which the Lord spoke in the face of His death: "Unless the grain of wheat falls into the ground and dies, it remains alone . . ."

The more we are resolved to follow in the imitation of our Lord, the more will charity grow in us, and it will expand into a power nothing can withstand.

Our generation has a frightening responsibility. Developments everywhere are pressing toward world unity, toward a consolidation of all the advances mankind has achieved during recent years, toward a union of all nations. Already, every point on earth can be reached by plane, by radio, by television—but also by weapons. The fateful question for ours and the coming generation is this: Will this one world that is in the making be Christian or anti-Christian?

Only a united and renewed Christianity, living out of the fullness of revealed Christian truth, can withstand the onrush of the anti-Christ.

Only a united and renewed Christianity will be able to cope with the immense missionary tasks posed by the awakened nations of Africa and Asia.

With our human eyes we cannot discern any way in which the unification of Christendom can come about in the near future. Only God can work the miracle of a new Pentecost even in our day, but God needs men who are willing, like Mary and the first disciples were willing, to be made new by the spirit of Pentecost.

To make ourselves ever more ready for this hour is the task to which we were called by Pope John and by the council—the council which was "an invitation to all Christians to seek and to achieve that unity for which Jesus Christ implored his heavenly Father with such ardent prayers."